FOOTSTEPS
IN THE
PAST

MARGARET MOXOM

authorHOUSE®

AuthorHouse™ UK
1663 Liberty Drive
Bloomington, IN 47403 USA
www.authorhouse.co.uk
Phone: 0800.197.4150

Published by AuthorHouse 06/30/2018

ISBN: 978-1-5462-9443-6 (sc)
ISBN: 978-1-5462-9444-3 (e)

Print information available on the last page.

CONTENTS

Alternative Ending

My special thanks go to Roy for checking
the Potteries dialect for me and my partner
for proof-reading the manuscript.

En.wikipedia.org

CHAPTER 1

The first time I saw the Lodge entrance to Ash Hall it totally took me aback, so incongruous to the rest of the buildings surrounding it on Ash Bank Road, which were 20th century - and so unexpected – peeking out at a slight angle to the main road so catching your eye as you drove up from through Bucknall from Hanley. This lodge looked back to a time and style of long ago, in fact, further back than when the lodge was actually built, as it was built in a most impressive, dark and foreboding gothic style, made of ashlar stone, with a slate roof and elaborate verge parapets. It was just a small building, containing just two rooms, originally with just a tiny storeroom at the rear, but an extension being added on in the mid 1800s. It was originally built for the coachman and groom at Ash Hall. There is a crest carved in blackened sandstone of a lion rampant above the main door. The windows are lead-lined in a diamond pattern. Funnily enough, looking around, you can see that a lot of the newer buildings have these diamond pattern windows, which, to my mind, was a means of keeping some form of connection, no matter how vague, to the design of the lodge.

At the side of the lodge are an ornate set of black and gold gates fronting a red gravelled drive flanked on either side by monkey puzzle trees.

This drive leads to Ash Hall itself – an amazing structure. I remember standing there, looking up at it in all its glory and thinking to myself, "what a wonderful place to work". It was a mansion completed by Job Meigh, in the same style as the lodge, on 27 March 1837 – there is the date "1837" on the rainwater heads on the front of the building. The architecture is a work of beauty. The exterior is of hard ash-coloured stone, obtained from the estate grounds. The oriel windows are surmounted with pointed gables. An elegant portico, composed of three Gothic arches, turreted and embattled, adorns the front. The adjoining lawn is tastefully laid out and planted; altogether, Ash Hall must be one of the most beautiful buildings built at the time.

Ash Hall: Steve Birks, www.thepotteries.org

The mansion is now a Grade ll listed nursing home caring for older people with physical difficulties or dementia and can accommodate 61 resid in 39 single and 11 shared rooms (14 en-suite) with the option for overnight visitors to stay.

I was 25 and just moved up from London. Of course, I'd come there for an interview, not to admire the scenery.

Anyway, I got the job, as a care assistant, which included basically assisting residents and staff with meals, distribution of medication, washing and dressing residents, bed baths and turning for end of life patients, to prevent bed sores, dealing with visitors' questions, assisting patients with any needs or requests, taking them for wheelchair walks, gathering patients for entertainment shows or exercise, basic observation and anything else that is deemed necessary under my remit, depending what shift I was on. I had attended various courses on rehabilitation of stroke victims, which I was interested in developing further. The people who interviewed me at the nursing home were interested in this and said they would give me a trial but finances were not available at present for a full-time stroke victim therapist. I accepted this, on the understanding that, should a post become available elsewhere, I would apply for it but would be grateful for the opportunity to practise my newly-acquired skills at Ash Hall.

Obviously, the Hall has been modified considerably, with the addition of an 8-person lift and specially equipped bathing facilities. There are three lounges equipped with flat-screen digital TV viewing, three dining rooms for small group-dining, with an activities co-ordinator offering a full activity programme, with artists attending frequently to entertain, and hair salon and trips out.

CHAPTER 2

It was time for the evening meal. Most residents in the dining room were capable of feeding themselves but obviously a few needed help.

"Hello, Mrs Hyslop, do you need any help today."

"Yes, ducky, I can't cut up the meat. Can you give me a hand".

While doing so, I chatted along with her. "And how are you today, have you done anything interesting?"

"Not really, one of the nurses took me out into the garden in my wheelchair, it's a lovely day, just a slight breeze blowing. You know, it's a lovely view. So different from when I was a kid. You could see far and wide from the top of Ash Bank Road – then it was all chimneys and smoke over Hanley way and Etruria. You could see the smoke just hovering there, choking the atmosphere. Not a nice place then. But so much has changed, for the better I might add, there's only one chimney stack down there now that I can see. That's still billowing out smoke"

"Yes, you must have memories, good and bad, of the Potteries."

"Yes, I was a potter, well not actually a potter, but it was my job to paint the pots at Royal Doulton in Nile

Street, Burslem. Of course, when I was a kid, quite a few of the pottery businesses had closed down, so I didn't see the worst of it."

"That's very interesting, Mrs Hyslop, and I will get back to this, but I hope you don't mind, I see that Mr Cholerton needs a hand".

"That's fine ducky, I'm not going anywhere".

"I'll just help you with that Mr Cholerton."

"Thank you, can't seem to steady my hands". Mr Cholerton had Parkinsons so I cut up his food into smaller portions, loaded a fork and fed him, taking care to wipe his mouth after each mouthful, as the Parkinsons made him dribble.

"Were you ever involved in the Potteries, Mr Cholerton, it's just that Mrs Hyslop was saying she was a painter."

"Well yes, I suppose most of us were at some time or another. I was a potter, worked for Wedgwoods in Etruria until 1950, when the factory closed down. It's now the site of Bet 365. I then went to work for 'Beswicks' in Longton. It was a different time then and we actually had a visit, would you believe it, from the Queen, that was an honour, and Cilla Black visited us in the 1970s. It was like a big family with three generations of families working there. Where there were numerous members of the same family on the board, we called them by their first names, calling them Mr Basis or Mr James to distinguish between them."

"Aye, I was at Royal Doulton's 'Minton's' pottery", piped in Mrs Clarke, who was sitting opposite, "when Les Dawson came to visit in September 1982. He was a laugh, he said we were 'the thinking man's Wedgwood', sorry and all that, Mr Cholerton, but that's what he said. Such a scream, he complimented the management on the spotlessness of the 'Minton' canteens, saying: 'You could eat off the floor in here. You have to – the tables are filthy'. That was just his way. We also had Workers' Playtime, that started back in the 40s, to cheer up the workers during the war years. They brought it back in 1982, so we could work to pop music. Such a laugh, with all us girls singing as we worked. Anyway, getting back to Les Dawson, you remember he was famous for his mother-in-law jokes, well he joked that his mother-in-law had arrived, saying she caused the mice to throw themselves into the traps! He then added that there were no mice in the canteen'cos the rats had eaten them all!"

"So, it wasn't so bad" I cut in.

"Oh, it was damned hard work" replied Mr Cholerton, "but a lot better than the previous century, that wasn't a time to be alive. We had unions and proper pay and benefits when I was there. Obviously I wasn't around in the 1800s, although I might look like it, (he laughed) but it's in the history books – you'll need to look up all about the Pottery riots."

"If you're really interested and want to know more, I tell you who could give you an insight", interrupted Mrs Hyslop, "Mr Shenton over there... he used to be a history teacher. He can't remember what he did five minutes ago, but he still knows his history teaching. If you're really interested, he might be able to help".

"Yes, unfortunately he doesn't know who I am from one day to the next but, if I get a chance, I'll see what he remembers."

After dinner was over I thought I'd take advantage of talking to Mr Shenton.

Mr Shenton was slumped in an armchair, staring into space, even though the TV was on. He seemed to be withdrawn into himself, in his own thoughts, or maybe there were no thoughts, just an emptiness. There was no expression on his face. I approached him cautiously so as not to startle him. "Mr Shenton", I whispered, "Mr Shenton". There was a slight response, a turn of his head to one side. "Mr Shenton, may I speak with you". He turned towards me, a sort of blankness in his eyes as if he were not really focusing, then slowly he looked up at me. "Mr Shenton, how do you do, my name is Jane, I'm one of your nurses here at the Ash Hall Nursing Home". I'd told him this many times now but, unfortunately, his dementia wouldn't allow him to retain this information.

"Can I help you?" he replied, slowly.

"I hope you can, Mr Shenton. I was told that you used to be a history teacher". I didn't say the name of the person who told me as the name wouldn't mean anything to him and would only confuse him even more. His eyes flickered as if he were trying to recall something, something deep in his past.

"Yes, I am a history teacher. I work at the Moorfields High School. I really don't know why I am here. Have I been ill?"

"You'll be here for a while, Mr Shenton. However, as you are a history teacher, I wondered if you could help me with the history of the Potteries. I'm very interested, specifically in the riots of 1842."

There was a light slowly becoming evident in his eyes, a sort of awakening and he smiled. "OK, class, sit down, today we're going to concentrate on the lead up to the Pottery riots of 1842." he said in a commanding voice and stood up to face me, as I sat down.

I'd brought a notepad and pen with me on the off chance I could get through to him.

He commenced. "This time in the history of the Potteries was a turbulent period. The 19th century factory conditions were probably worse than anything you'll find in Charles Dickens. Put simply, they were hellish. In 1861 there were 4,000 children under the age of 10, working full time in the industry. Of these, nearly 600 were aged only five years. Can you imagine that class? What were you doing when you were five years old?

"At infants school, learning to read and write." I replied.

"Yes, most definitely, but were you also doing back-breaking toil for 12 hours or more a day in close proximity to a smouldering furnace with hardly any food to sustain you?

"Certainly not, sir." I replied, "That's atrocious and doesn't bear thinking about."

"Yes, when you were five class, you went to school from 9am to 3pm. You had a hot lunch provided and were able to play outside in the break times. At the end of school you were picked up by your mother and taken home to a nice tea, watched TV or played with friends and family. Then you'd be tucked up in a nice warm bed and read a story before going to sleep. You boys probably dreamed of becoming an astronaut or footballer or even a pop star. I don't know what you girls dreamed of, probably being a princess.

These poor kids were just trying to survive - children of the same age were already starting a working life of back-breaking toil and hardship – and those were just the lucky ones.

Draconian laws and a lack of child protection meant that children could easily be exploited in the workplace.

But in an age when most working class people were living in large families struggling on the breadline, there was no option but to send youngsters, under the age of 10, out to work.

What led up to families living in such poverty and starvation were the hated Corn Laws. I suggest you read Shaw's autobiography, 'When I Was A Child', as it gives us a first-hand account of what it was like to work in a pottery factory around 1840. Charles Shaw was a Methodist minister, who had been a child potter himself."

I made note of this in my notebook.

"When Victoria came to the throne, work was scarce and food was dear. The Corn Laws were bringing into play their most cruel and evil results, one being that little children had to compete for the decreasing sum of available work. There was no Factory Act at the time in the area, so the work of children was a harsh necessity. What you also might like to read, class, is John Abberley's 'Salute to the Potteries'."

I wrote that down too. Mr Shelton continued.

"The hated Corn Laws, to put them as succinctly as possible, were tariffs and restrictions on imported food and grain enforced in Great Britain between 1815 and 1846. They were designed to keep grain prices high to favour domestic producers and represented British mercantilism."

"Sorry, sir," I interrupted, "British mercantilism – I don't understand the term".

"Yes, mm… there was two industries, the landowners, dealing in agriculture and the industrialists. The landowners were Conservative and the industrialists, Whigs. To continue, the Corn Laws imposed steep import duties, making it too expensive to import grain from abroad. This seemed like a good idea at the time - that is, until food supplies were short, such as the Irish famine, when people were starving – they couldn't afford bread. They were meant to improve the profits of the land-owners. Food prices were kept high, hence, the cost of living rose. However, for the workers on low wages, food came first, which meant other manufacturing industries were losing out. The Whig industrialists opposed the Conservative landlords.

The Corn Laws stated that it would be dangerous for Britain to rely on imported corn because lower prices would reduce labourers' wages and manufacturers would lose out, due to the decrease of purchasing power of landlords and farmers. They wanted corn kept to 80 shillings a quarter, which was unobtainable. After the war ended in 1814 corn prices decreased. Tory, Lord Liverpool, passed the Corn Law in 1815 to keep the price of bread high. This resulted in serious rioting in London.

The Corn Laws were repealed by Prime Minister, Sir Robert Peel, a Conservative, with the support of the Whigs and overcoming the opposition of most of his party. On 25 June 1846 the Duke of Wellington got it passed through the House of Lords, attributing the success to Richard Cobden, who, together with John Bright, founded the Anti-Corn Law League.

OK, class, any questions?"

"So, how I understand it, sir, a tariff was put on imported grain, the price of grain was kept high to aid the landowners as they thought workers' wages would suffer, but, as wages were low anyway, the manufacturers lost out, as the workers' money was spent on food and they couldn't afford any other products. Then starvation set in when supply of grain was reduced, due to weather conditions and bad harvests."

"Sorry, to interrupt, but could you please expand on how did this lead to the riots of 1842." I ventured.

"Yes, mm, let me think, yes…. The ongoing depression led factory owners to cut wages two or three times between 1840 and June 1842. Each occasion prompted scattered strikes and protestations, but the wave of cuts continued. The beginning of continuous striking occurred on 18 July 1842, actually in Hanley. Trade unions were illegal in Britain, although unions were well-established in many locations. A group of miners assembled and swore not to resume work until wages and working conditions were bettered. As the strike spread to the other coalfields of Staffordshire, the strikers in Hanley and elsewhere passed resolutions in support of the People's Charter while maintaining their original wage-related demands. Strikers spread the campaign by marching from town to town and collecting their fellow labourers.

Despite the workers' best efforts at legitimacy, reports in the upper-class newspaper, 'The Guardian', characterised the workers as a lawless mob. Strike leaders were portrayed as dirty, cowardly and treacherous. In London, Home Secretary, Sir James Graham, readied artillery and troops were dispatched towards Lancashire on 13 August. On this same date, Queen Victoria issued an edict, declaring the illegality of the strikes and offering a £50 reward for turning in a fellow striker. Although some labourers earned on £5 a month, few chose to desert the campaign."

Mr Shelton continued, "Even though the region around Manchester was paralysed, the strikes did not become truly national in scope until the National Charter Association, aka the Chartists, officially endorsed the campaign on 16 August, immediately helping spread the strikes further. They demanded universal male suffrage, the eligibility of all classes to be a Member of Parliament and other political reforms."

"Sorry, what was universal male suffrage" I interrupted. "I've heard naturally of the Suffragettes, for votes for women but not male suffrage."

"Well, class, this is a little known fact that has been swept under the carpet, so to say. As you rightly say, woman didn't have the vote at the time, nor, in fact, did any man who did not own a property and, as most properties in the area were rented, only the landowners had the vote. Basically, as these landowners were Tories, out to make as much money for themselves as possible, not caring a fig for their workers, they didn't want their workers to get the Tories out of power. Now, if that answers your question, I'll continue......, now where was I, ok.... as well as the north of England, parts of South Wales, Scotland, Dorset and Somerset now joined the strike. 500,000 workers remained on strike through the end of August and into September. On 29 August some factories attempted to reopen, but the number of labourers who showed up to work numbered in the tens. As food became harder to come by in September, some workers did return for a week, get paid, and then leave again, the most perseverant holding out until the end of September. In all cases, strikers prevented proposed wage cuts at their factories. Some had to settle with this small victory, in other cases owners granted wage increases from pre-strike levels. So, although the campaign did not succeed in passing the Charter, the initial goal of better pay was achieved.

"Yes, that's about it in a nutshell. So, class dismissed."

Mr Shelton then seemed to return to his former self. He became weak and sat down. His eyes glazed over again. "My wife is supposed to be visiting today, have you seen her?"

I knew that Mr Shelton's wife had passed away some years before, so he has reverted and his dementia taken over. Just then a middle-aged lady walked into the dining room and headed towards us.

"There she is, hello Ruth." – Unfortunately, the middle-aged lady was his daughter. I took the opportunity to depart, the poor lady would have to deal with Mr Shelton's dementia in her own way.

I should have gone home ages ago. The sun was beginning to set with a beautiful red sunset. I went upstairs to collect my things and to see the sunset in its full majesty. It was quite quiet on the landing, everyone was either in their rooms or watching TV or playing board games downstairs. All of a sudden I heard a series of loud cracks outside and shouting, that appeared to be coming from directly below me. I peered out of the window but could see nothing. Then, a vague figure of a man appeared running away from the house. He seemed to be staggering, almost falling at times. I watched him run in the direction of the moors, then disappear.

I ran downstairs and out the front door. I could see nothing – there was no-one outside. Everything was still, nothing broken. Molly, a nurse, was at the reception. "Molly,

I've just seen a man running away from the house towards the moors and heard a lot of noise, cracks and shouting."

"You're imagining things, Jane. I've heard nothing, just the normal sounds coming from the lounge. Did you see anything outside just then?"

"No, there's no-one there. Are you sure one of the patients hasn't decided to take some exercise in the grounds?"

"No, they're all either tucked up in their rooms or in the lounge. They're all here, present and correct and no-one has passed me. In any case, you said you saw a man running, come on, do you think any of our patients could actually run?"

"Yes, you're right."

"Tell you what it could be, maybe someone is on the moors, shooting hares. The sound of the gun could have reverberated against the windows. That'll be it."

"Possibly, but that doesn't explain the man running away from the house."

"Well, maybe you've seen a ghost.....huuuuuu huuuuuu (making ghost-like sounds, then laughing). Come on Jane, you've had a long day and your mind is playing tricks on you. What are you still doing here at this time anyway? Be off with you and I'll see you tomorrow, bright and refreshed and no more talk of ghosts and ghoulies."

"OK, Molly. I'm going. See you tomorrow."

CHAPTER 3

I managed to get hold of Charles Shaw's "When I Was A Child". The hardships adults and children had to face in the 19th century really brought a tear to my eye, and I got quite engrossed looking on line and in libraries to find out more about the age.

A week or so later, I was just going off shift for the weekend but taking a final look around to see that everything was in order and no-one needed attention. I was walking along an upstairs corridor, peeping into the rooms, checking everyone was OK when a very strange feeling came over me. I felt a bit faint and the corridor started spinning. I had to hold onto the wall to steady myself. I closed my eyes as I began to feel nausea, a sort of sea-sickness. After what seemed like an eternity, but was probably only a few minutes, I felt calmer and opened my eyes.

The normally well-lit, decorated corridor had changed. It was now a dark, wood-panelled area, lit by gas lamps. The carpet had gone – there were just the floorboards. Where was I, what had happened? A feeling of panic came over me. I felt like screaming out for help but my brain stopped me – who would be out there to help me – maybe no-one, maybe someone dangerous? I then looked down at what I was wearing. I had been wearing my nurses uniform. What I had on now was a dark striped bodice with slight puff sleeves, a dark long coarse linen skirt that gathered at the waist and ballooning out, reaching to my ankles. A long white apron was tied around my waist. Under the skirt were a couple of long petticoats, that's all. I felt my hair – it was tied up and covered by a white bonnet affair and what felt like a cotton frill all the way round at the front. I couldn't put an age to the style but definitely 19th century or even earlier.

Someone was playing a joke on me, was my next thought. Either that or I had fallen asleep, maybe exhausted after a long shift and fainted and I was dreaming. I'll wake up in a minute. I tried pinching myself. It hurt, but I was still there in this dark corridor in this strange outfit.

I looked out of the nearest window. What I saw below was a man chopping wood. The sleeves of his shirt were rolled up to the elbows. He had dark, baggy, possibly corduroy, trousers on and a thick leather belt around his waist. He looked in his early to mid- 30s. His hair was fairish with a slight curl. It was over his ears. He was well built and, I presumed had rippling muscles underneath that shirt. I watched him as he raised his axe on a stump of wood, brought it down and placed a chopped off piece upright again to bring the axe down on it again, chopping the wood into smaller pieces. He looked sweaty and a bit grubby, but I supposed he would be, doing that sort of work.

Just then, I heard a clatter and rumble – it sounded like something was coming along the path to the right. A horse's head appeared, harnessed to and hauling a covered carriage – an 18th or 19th century carriage, something straight out of Jane Austen's 'Pride and Prejudice'.

I know, I thought to myself. I must have been to sleep and now I've woken up and they're staging an enactment of one of Jane Austen's novels here or some other historic novel, with actors in costume. It's the right setting, but strange no-one bothered to tell me. Where are the cameras?

A man got out of the carriage. He was well-dressed for the time, slim with chiselled features. His costume consisted of tight breaches, a waistcoat, a short-wasted jacket, with tails, a white shirt with a high collar, with a sort of white cravatte wrapped around the collar. He was wearing a dark hat, not a stove hat like Isambard Kingdom Brunel, shorter but not exactly a bowler. I would say he was about 58 or 59.

"I'm back, Woods. Tell Weston to take the carriage to the stable and rub down the horse. Get some good oats for her. Be quick about it or you'll feel my whip."

"Yes, sir." replied the woodman, whose surname was obviously Woods - but who was the smartly-dressed fellow meant to be? It could be an enactment of 'Lady Chatterley's Lover', what with the woodman, come gamekeeper.

I decided to go downstairs. The whole place had changed. Yes, the beautifully carved, oak, resplendent staircase was still there, but no patients, no nurses or doctors. There was no reception desk. The dining room with elderly armchairs and tables and a TV for the patients was gone. The room was now beautifully furnished with a long, highly polished table, set with candelabra and many chairs, a huge matching, highly carved sideboard, other matching pieces of heavy, ornate furniture, presumably for storage and a high set of drawers, plus some plush armchairs and a leather, studded settee. On the walls were paintings of portraits, framed in ornate gold frames, of ladies and gentlemen in 18th or 19th century costumes and smaller country scenes paintings.

I made my way down the stairs only to be confronted by the well-tailored gentleman.

"Who are you? He sternly asked. Before I could answer (not that I knew what to say), he continued, "Oh you must be the one who answered the advertisement for a new assistant for my wife. Our previous one just up and left. These fly-by-nights just keep coming and going. They don't stay long – frightened of a good days' work. Well they should thank their lucky stars they're not labouring in the pits or the potteries. Come on then wench, what's your name?"

"Jane" I replied, stuttering a bit, "Jane Paget".

"Jane Paget, Sir, if you please, otherwise you'll be out on your ear in no time".

"Sorry, Sir." I replied.

"Right, your duties will be to attend on me and my wife for whatever requirements we need and to help my wife with her hair and dressing. Unfortunately, she had an accident early on this year and is not the person she used to be. So she needs assistance. Just to warn you, she can be a bit temperamental now and forgetful, but you're to treat her kindly. You will also be required to serve our meals at table and keep the rooms tidy and clean. We have a cook, Dinah Chetwynd and assistant, Harriet Jones, who also makes up the fires, does the washing, makes up the beds, beats the carpets, empties the commodes and everything else. We have a handyman and gardener, John Woods, and Joseph Weston, who is the coachman and groom, who lives in the Lodge at the entrance to the drive. I expect my morning newspaper at 7am, with my breakfast. Bring the post in when it arrives. I quite often have important guests, who will dine with us. I expect you to be courteous and be at their beck and call. As you may know, I am a magistrate. Anything you hear is in confidence and must not be repeated out of this house. Do you understand? And if I find out that information has been passed on, God help you, my girl!"

"Yes, Sir". I curtseyed, somehow or other I felt it was called for, although I'd never curtseyed in my life.

"By the way, your accent's not from here. Where to you hail from."

"London Sir." I didn't know where to say exactly as I had no idea what was going on in London in the 18th or 19th centuries. Maybe the area I lived in didn't exist then, but fortunately he didn't quiz me further.

"Hmm. OK, go to your duties, I'm sure cook will be able to instruct you."

What the heck had I got myself into? It was dawning on me that this whole set-up was real. I had to find out what year I was in.

I went toward where I knew the modern day kitchen was. Dinah Chetwynd was there and introduced myself. The kitchen had a long wooden bench in the middle with tons of copper saucepans and cooking utensils around the walls and floor and wall cabinets and a huge Butler sink with wooden draining board. On one wall was a large wood-burning stove. It also had numerous gas hobs, so obviously, gas was being piped in, for the lights in the hallways and rooms too. Mrs Chewynd was busy preparing something.

"When was this house built?" I ventured to Dinah.

"Oh, the Master bought the estate in '37 and started building this 'all then. 'him and the Mistress 'as only moved in last year. There's still work to be done on some of the rooms and out'ouses. All mod cons 'ere - these gas contraptions are brilliant but you 'ave to be very careful 'ow you uses them. I'm frightened the 'ole thing's gonna blow up. Not really my cuppa tea. Saying that, do you want a cuppa?"

"That's alright, Mrs Chetwynd".

"We've got running water too, straight into the sink over there." I don't know I'm born, no fetching buckets of water from a standpipe 'ere, not like down in the smoke. It's very good water and it's laid on for some of 'is tenants too. You don't 've to boil it but the only thing is it does leave a lot of lime in the kettle."

The Master and Mistress also 'as water pumped up to their closets and, begging your pardon, and all that, but a stools pot as well. A beautifully ornate china pot with a wooden seat with a hole in it. You sit on the seat, do your business then you turns a handle and water comes down a pipe from a little tank above and flushes it all away out the back of it into a larger pipe with an 'S'-shaped bend and an 'inged flap at the base of the pan, which, I've been told stops the smells coming back to 'aunt yer - then the pipe disappears underground. Mr Meigh said it's something to do with, what did 'e call it, yes 'gravity'. I've never seen nowt like it. All the latest gadgets 'as our Mr Meigh, even afore it's on the market. O' course, the likes of us has to make do with the out'ouse.

"How nice Mrs Chetwynd." I replied, pondering how someone could be so over the moon about running water and toilets. I must get a date, find out what year I'm in. "You don't, by chance, have an old paper, one the Master has thrown out, do you?"

"Oh, you can read. That's good. I never really learnt. Anyway, there might be one in the coal scuttle over there, ready to make the fire with."

I was in luck, there was a screwed up paper. I scoured it for a date – it was Friday, 9th May, 1842…. Jesus, I'm in the 19th Century, I almost said aloud, but stopped myself in time. Victoria would be on the throne, just about – round about that time anyway. The paper was 'The Northern Star'. The front page concerned a second petition of over three million signatures being submitted to Parliament! 'The Northern Star' commented on the rejection:

"Three and a half millions have quietly, orderly, soberly, peaceably but firmly asked of their rulers to do justice; and their rulers have turned a deaf ear to that protest. Three and a half millions of people have asked permission to detail their wrongs, and enforce their claims for RIGHT, and the 'House' has resolved they should not be heard! Three and a half millions of the slave-class have holden out the olive branch of peace to the enfranchised and privileged classes and sought for a firm and compact union, on the principle of EQUALITY BEFORE THE LAW; and the enfranchised and privileged have refused to enter into a treaty! The same class is to be a slave class still. The mark and brand of inferiority is not be removed. The assumption of inferiority is still to be maintained. The people are not to be free."

This meant nothing to me. Obviously, a petition had gone to Parliament for the rights of the 'slave-class' and the petition had been rejected – but who were the 'slave-class'. I hadn't heard anything about this in my history classes at school. I didn't want to pursue this at the moment but, obviously, to get onto the front page of a newspaper, there must be something drastic going on. I didn't want to bring this up with Mrs Chetwynd, not just now anyway, it could wait, I needed to find out further about Mr Meigh. He was obviously the owner of Ash House in the 19th Century, the same house that is now a nursing home.

"Mrs Chetwynd, can you tell me anything about the Master. Anything I should know. I wasn't told much, I don't even know his full name."

"Well, ducky, as long as you minds your Ps and Qs and keeps your nose to the grindstone, you'll be alright. 'Cos he can be a bit of a bounder. 'e doesn't stand fools, if you knows what I mean and 'e's not afraid to lash out, not just with 'is tongue."

"He said he's a magistrate".

"Yes, ducky. 'igh and mighty our Mr Job Meigh the 2nd is. He used to have the pottery works, 'icks, Meigh and Johnson, off 'untsbach Street in 'anley, but that went by the by in '35. 'e left there a very rich man, that's how 'e managed to buy this estate. 'h owns all the farm around 'ere. – Little Ash Farm, Big Ash Farm, Ash House, Sherwins at Five Lanes Ends, Metal 'ouse, Bleach 'ouse in Washerwall, 'anley 'ayes Farm, Brook'ouse Farm, Stuarts, and they all pays him rent. Those tenants who've got children always have sweets in a parcel to take 'ome as a treat for 'em. 'e'd gone into partnership with a Richard 'icks, who is married to his sister, Lydia and a Mr Johnson, who I believe is related to his wife, though I may have got that wrong. I know 'e started out as a rep for 'em anyway. Anyway, 'e's a well-'onoured man and has medals for his work from the Society of hArts as 'e got managed to get rid of the poisons in the glazes used on the pottery pieces, so 'e needs to be well respected. I don't know if you've seen in the grounds but 'e's made little pools along the stream, and a water wheel. 'ere he mixes 'is colours in the little ponds for using on his pots."

"That's very interesting, Mrs Chetwynd."

She continued, seemed to want to tell all and I wasn't complaining, the more I knew the better informed I'd be. "'e's the Deputy Lieutenant of the County, 'e is, and County Magistrate, the Master's a Trustee of 'anley Market and 'ad a lot to do with the building of the Town 'all. The mistress came from the Mellor family, Elizabeth, daughter of William Mellor, who 'as the pottery in Charles Street. Unfortunately, she doesn't keep too good nowadays since the accident and needs a bit of 'elp doing things. I expects that's why you're 'ere."

"Yes, the Master mentioned briefly about the accident and that I would be her maid, as well as doing various other tasks."

The Master's son lives here too, on and off – William Mellor Meigh – that's where 'e gets his double name from, 'is mother, so combining the 'ouses, with his wife Eliza. They married in '37 and have a one-year-ol' son, also called William Mellor Meigh an' a three-year-old daughter, Elizabeth. The Master's son farms hAsh Farm. They also 'ave hAsh House, at the end of the drive, over hAsh Bank Road. Fer what I can gather, they intend on pulling the old building down and rebuilding. I don't know when that's going to happen though."

"Well thank you Mrs Chetwynd, that's most informative. You must have been with the Master a long time?"

"Yes, ducky, I moved 'ere with him fer where 'e was 'fore

at Bank 'ouse, Shelton. As I said, nose to the grindstone and you'll be alright. So, you'd better get to business. It's time for the Master's supper. 'ere, take it into him."

The Mistress was not in the dining room so I returned to the kitchen for her meal. I knocked on the door and was greeted by a weak voice. On entering I saw a lady whom, I would say, was in her late 50s. She was sitting at the dressing table either staring into space or deep in thought. Her hair was unkempt. It should have been in a bonnet but was loosely tied with strands hanging down. She had on what looked like a nightdress with a shawl wrapped around her. I noticed that there was a walking cane propped up at the dressing table.

"I have your tea, Mrs Meigh. I'll put it on the table. I am your new maid, Jane. Do you wish any assistance?"

She turned her head round slowly towards me and tried to smile and I could see immediately that she had suffered some sort of a stroke as her smile was lopsided. "Do you wish me to help you to the table?"

The smile faded. She answered, very slowly and deliberately but with a slur to her voice "I'm quite…capable, I'm… not…an invalid." She made a grab for the cane but missed and it fell on the floor. I sped over to pick it up and helped her stand up. Her left arm was limp and fell as she attempted to stand, so, obviously, the stroke had affected her left side.

"Leave… me …be, I don't …need …your assistance."

"I'm sorry if I am being forward but please be assured I am here to help you. I have plenty of experience working with people who have been involved in accidents, or the elderly, and can provide an exercise regime and massage

26

to try to get muscles working that have been subjected to neurological damage, such as in the cases of strokes."

"Oh, …… so I see you're edu…cated. The maids I've had ….before haven't even been able…. to read. Anyway, ….I don't need any … help, maybe neaten my hair and help me dress, when necessary, as …. befits a maid. There's nothing …. wrong with me, so just leave the meal …. you can go now."

"Well, let's try to eat something first and then we'll talk. Maybe I can tidy your hair after your meal."

Mrs Meigh tried to stand again, but sat down again, rather awkwardly. I caught her, to save her from falling.

"Let me be, you impudent girl. My leg has just…….. gone to sleep. I must have … been ….sitting too long."

"Mrs Meigh. I can see that you are in denial. But you have had a stroke following your accident. You're having difficulty walking and your left arm has no muscle tone. I can help you regain your balance and movement with set exercises. If you'll let me help you. Just let me see you raise your left arm."

"Oh, I'm just tired. I'll be …..better ….. in a minute."

"Sorry, I'm not going. Now, raise your left arm" I repeated, more as an order than before.

"Did you say something, girl, I was thinking of other things?"

Yes, I thought to myself, that's another symptom of a stroke, not being able to concentrate, but I'm not going to give up.

"Come, Mrs Meigh, your dinner is getting cold. I'll help you to the table." And I raised her up and supported her. Her left foot was dragging but we got the few steps to the table and I sat her down, cut up her food for her and watched as she loaded her fork with her right hand.

While she was eating I made small talk, getting away from her physical problems and talking about her family. She seemed to becoming more at ease with me so, after a while I managed to get onto the subject of the 'accident'.

It seems she'd had the "accident" in February. She was descending from the carriage and fell, hitting her head on the frozen ground. Some weeks had passed before she finally became aware of her surroundings, then found that she could hardly speak and could not move her left arm and her left leg would not support her.

I told her it sounded like a brain haemorrhage, which had caused the stroke. I added that plenty of people have made startling recoveries, with good medical attention and the assistance of physiotherapists and speech therapists.

"Sorry, I ... don't understand. What is that term, 'physio… therapist'. I've never heard… the word."

Thinking about the year, 1842, I had to restrain my explanation and just said, "I trained in London. We have doctors and hospitals there looking into injuries of the brain. Obviously this is a newly formed specialised field of medicine and has not migrated yet to the countryside. Physiotherapy can aid repair to muscles and nerves with gentle, repeated exercise, which we can do together. How often do you get to go out?"

"Oh… it's too much…. too difficult … so I stay here."

"Do you have a wheelchair?"

"What is… a wheelchair….. oh, I see, a chair on wheels, you mean… a Bath chair. Yes, Mr Meigh got one, …a sort of …wickerwork chair, two wheels …at the back …and one …attached …to a… oh I can't remember, oh… a steering column, that's it. But I'm not able ….to steer it, so it's …useless. It's in the coach … house, but I can't …get down… the stairs."

"That's OK. I'm sure John will be able to fix up some sort of device to lower you downstairs. I'll have a work with him and about the, er…Bath chair."

It was dark now, so I decided to seek out John the next day.

I found John tending to the flowers and lawns and introduced myself. I approached the subject of possibly getting some form of hoist to enable the Mistress to descend the stairs. He came up with a few ideas and did some sketches, which looked possible.

"Tha's a place arint bek o' steers o' maybe aside o' steers, thah knowst, as'll day. Ah cud put up a pullah thar, hong et far t'sailing. Ah'll mizzer up, say what way con day. Eet'll bay a friggling job but ah'll ev a go ducky."

"Sorry, John, I'm having a bit of trouble understanding your dialect", I interrupted, "Mrs Chetwynd is easier to understand."

"Ah thet wud bay 'cos ah coms fer th Potteries, Mrs Chetwynd started owt t'other sade o' Newcassle. Eet'll com bay en bay, the mer thay spakes te may".

Anyway, there was an area to the side of the main staircase, where a pulley could be erected. Come to think of it, I thought to myself, this was where the lift is at the nursing home. John would have to have a word with the Master to see if he would agree and pay for the work and equipment, but, if the Master agreed, a pulley could be hooked to a ceiling beam and a rope attached to a chair with sides and a removable safety bar at the front, to lower the chair down. His idea was to cut a hole through the floor to one side of the top of the stairs, allowing width for the chair and passenger to descend to the ground floor. This hole could be covered by a wooden panel that would slide into place. So, when the chair was raised, the wooden panel would be slid into place to allow the passenger to place their feet on the panel to be able to rise from the chair and step away. The chair would be raised and lowered by a hand-operated lever attached to a winch. He said he'd work on the idea and also remove the driving column from the Bath chair. He had a rough accent and it was a bit difficult to understand him sometimes, though he was friendly enough. John said they use a similar system to lower people into the mines. Most were huge contraptions and much more complex as they had to lower cages containing horses down into the pits.

I began to wonder to myself if Mrs Meigh was the reason why I had been transported in time. If I managed to help her improve her situation and health, maybe then I'd be sent back to the future. There must be some reason why.

I was keeping an eye on the papers coming in to the house. Early in July I saw a column stating that a Mr Ridgway, Hanley's leading pottery manufacturer and chairman of the Stoke Board of Guardians, went on a deputation to see the Prime Minister. The deputation stated that, unless something was quickly done, he warned Peel "a struggle will commence of which no man can foresee the consequences".

I asked John if he knew anything of this Mr Ridgway.

"Yer, ah've 'erd ef 'im. Ay's a mon ov anuther cloth. Ah

belayve ay's well rispected. Eef ah rimember loik, it woz ay, oo abolished the truck system at 'is Ubberley pits nar 'anley. Ay paed fayre en 'ad a club fer seek workmen. Yer, ay's one ef th few good'uns."

CHAPTER 4

I started working with Mrs Meigh. Firstly I arranged to tie for her left boot, a string looping from the bottom of the lace to the top of the boot. The aim of this was to prevent 'foot drop', as the affected foot tends to drop after a stroke and if the boot is tied in this way, the foot is kept in one position and helps the patient walk. This made an immediate change to Mrs Meigh's walking ability as the left foot was now held and could be controlled to a certain extent. Mrs Meigh was really happy that such a simple device could have proved so helpful, plus it wouldn't be seen under her long skirts, and now began to trust me as I put her through a series of repetitive exercises to try to build up muscle tone in her left leg and arm.

It was extremely hard-going at first and Mrs Meigh easily got tired so we'd have a short break in between exercises and just talk, and I would listen patiently as she slowly formed what she was going to say.

During this time I'd not approached Mrs Meigh about the accident and how it had happened. I was leaving it to come up in conversation, but it never did. "Yes, I'd love to see my grandson, William, again. He was so chubby and giggly but I really did not feel able to see anyone and, as you know, I cut myself off from the outside world."

"That will change, and soon. You'll soon be out there again and be able to walk with your grandson."

"Yes, and I'd love to be able to walk in the gardens again and smell the flowers. They look so beautiful from my window."

She needed to be given an incentive. "Just keep on with the exercises, and you'll soon be able to do these things again. Wouldn't it be wonderful to see William again?"

"But it's so undignified doing these exercises, and I get so tired."

"No-one's watching you, only me. If you keep on doing the exercises, Mrs Meigh, you'll find they come easier and you won't feel so tired. You do want to walk again, unaided, now don't you?"

"Of course Jane, and I can see an improvement already. Thank you for your help."

With the exercises, she had to try to get her balance on one leg, while swinging the other out, then repeat with the other leg.

"Just hold tight to the table, Mrs Meigh. I'll be here to catch you should you wobble."

Mrs Meigh started off just doing the exercises in long night attire as there was no way that she could exercise in a tight bodice and multitudes of petticoats, as was the fashion then for ladies' daywear. It would have been better to wear some form of leggings but they didn't exist and she was very uncomfortable doing the floor exercises. I had an idea, though, and asked Dinah if she had a sewing machine. "Sorry ducky, we've no new-fangled machines like that 'ere.

Maybe in one of the factories but I've not 'eard the likes of anything. But, if yer wih, ah could possibly hand-sew a pair of loose cotton trousers, something like a man's pyjama, that would button in at the ankle, if that would serve?"

So, it seemed that sewing machines were still a long way off being manufactured. Anyway, Dinah produced a fine pair of loose trousers for Mrs Meigh to wear to do her exercises. We had a laugh about them as Mrs Meigh had never worn any form of trousers before. "What if someone were to see me. I'd be ridiculed?"

"Well, we'll have to make sure the door is locked. I'm certainly not going to tell anyone and nor will Dinah and what's a bit of indignity if it's getting you better?"

So, the exercises progressed, with Mrs Meigh continuing when I was not around.

I extracted a sash from one of Mrs Meigh's dresses, to use as a stirrup to go around each foot alternately, while lying on the floor, to raise the knee up, then pull the sash with the outer hand to turn the foot out, continuing to stretch the muscle. This would stretch the calf muscle and build coordination in the lower body and core muscles crucial to standing and walking

I explained to Mrs Meigh that these exercises needed to be practiced repetitively as each time you repeat an exercise, you strengthen the connections in the part of the brain that controls that movement. "The more you practice, the better you'll get."

I also devised arm and hand exercise such as holding coins in the hand and, using her index finger and thumb, work one coin at a time down onto the table.

After some weeks of these exercises, I brought in a set

of playing cards. "I've devised a little game that should be more interesting for you."

I spread out the playing cards, face down, on the table, each card in its own space.

"Now, this is a memory game as well as a hand and arm co-ordination game. We'll play together. You turn over two cards at a time, try to remember what they are, then turn them back again. Then you turn over another two cards each go. The plan is to find two matching cards – so, if you find a 10, try to remember if you've seen another 10 in the pack and where it was. You may find it difficult to pick up the cards but take your time. I want you to use your left hand. If you wish, you can use your right hand to guide and steady your left hand."

"Oh, I don't think…. I could do this, it sounds …too ….complicated."

"Nonsense, you'll enjoy it. We're in no rush, just take your time."

It was hard work at first but we continued and Mrs Meigh was gradually getting better.

I also showed her how to play a couple of Patience games, like Clock Patience, which she could amuse herself with when I was not present.

Singing is also a good exercise for speech development and we had fun singing nursery rhymes and songs that she knew such as doing a rondo together of "London's Burning".

"Oh Jane, I've not had such fun in a long time. I feel my enthusiasm for life returning, which I never dreamt possible."

"Yes, we'll soon have you out and about."

I was working with Mrs Meigh using the exercises I

had devised for her and speech therapy. I'd seen to her hair and helped her get dressed. It was a lovely, sunny day so I suggested we go out into the grounds, taking the bath chair if she needed it. I called John to help with the stair device he'd fixed up. Mrs Meigh had been a bit nervous, of course, when she had first used it, so I had sat in the chair myself with John operating the ropes, to show her that the chair was quite stable.

So, we went into the gardens. The flowers were in full bloom with fragrant aromas. John had done an excellent job there too.

I helped Mrs Meigh out of the bath chair and walked a little bit with her. I'd brought a child's ball to do a set of exercises with her – passing the ball from hand to hand, circling it around her body, first in a clockwise motion and then in an anti-clockwise motion. We had a laugh as she dropped the ball quite a few times, so it was good exercise for me to. We then practiced throwing to each other, initially just a few paces away then stepping out further. That was fun too, as the ball would go in any direction but we had a laugh about it.

After a little while I saw Mr Meigh approaching us.

"Good morning Jane. It's a beautiful day. I see my wife is making good strides with her exercises. Excuse me my love (speaking to Mrs Meigh) I would just like a short discussion with Jane." and we went a few yards away, leaving Mrs Meigh in her bathchair, enjoying the sunshine.

"I can see, even though you've only been here a short while, Jane, that Mrs Meigh is looking so much better and seems to be enjoying life again. That is such a good thing to see. You are good for her and the mechanism by the stairs, although quite preposterous to look at, is allowing her access to the gardens and sunshine. You have done well, Jane."

"Yes, Mrs Meigh is improving, sir, slowly but surely"

"Tell me, Jane, where did you learn this art?"

This was a difficult question, how could I answer it? I mean, Florence Nightingale hadn't even gone to the Crimea and women definitely weren't allowed into medical colleges. I had to think on my feet.

"Oh, I have a small group of lady friends, in London, who get together on a regular basis to discuss such things. Some of us have close relatives who have suffered to some degree or other, some form of palsy or weakness and, in our meetings, we have discussed and devised treatments, which have been tried on these relatives to some degree of success. We are all well-read, learned ladies, home taught." (I added). "My father wanted me to study, so have had private tutors for modern languages including the basics of Greek and Latin, plus other general subjects." I had a distinction in medical terminology, which took its bases from Greek and Latin, although I knew that didn't really count. I just wanted to impress him. I hoped he wasn't going to test me.

"So, your father is a man of substance?"

Again, I had to conjure up something quickly, "Oh yes, sir, papa is a lawyer in Lincoln's Inn Fields, London." Mr Meigh was obviously trying to ascertain whether or not I owned a property. I was thinking to myself that I owned a house in Werrington, to prove I had property, but that house wouldn't have been built yet, nor, to that end, would the old terraced house I had in London before moving to Staffordshire. That was Georgian, after Victoria had died and at the current time, Victoria had only just come to the throne.

"And does your father have premises?"

"Yes, he has a fairly substantial house off Chancery Lane, close by Lincoln's Inn, sir." (I lied)

"Are you an only child?"

"I am, Mr Meigh. I suppose, on the unfortunate demise of my parents, the house will revert to me. In the meantime, I am learning my trade as a carer for people with physical disabilities."

"Do you intend to marry at some future time, Jane?"

Again, an awkward question. I'd read the Brontës and Jane Austen, and seen the various film productions of their works on TV, so from what I understood, in this day and age, if I married, all my property and possessions would go to my husband and it would be in the hands of any husband to decide my fate, so I answered, "I do not intend to marry, sir. To forsake my inheritance could be a disastrous choice, plus I could succumb to a worse fate through child-bearing. It is not something I would like to consider at present, sir."

"So, Jane, you seem to have a hard head on your shoulders. I do not adhere to everything you say, but you may change your mind in the future, should you meet an upstanding, honest husband. However, for the time being we must consider ourselves fortunate to have such a well-read person with such abilities in our midst, someone of possible future good standing in the community."

"I thank you, sir." and bowed.

"I apologise, Jane, for this seemingly assault of questioning but it has been interesting finding out more about you."

"Not at all, sir".

Mr Meigh continued, "My wife and I have not been able to be social since her accident but, looking at the progress today that she has made, with your outstanding assistance, I might add, I believe it might be possible to arrange a little soirée with a few friends and acquaintances. I feel my wife would now like the opportunity for a social evening, as she has been so cocooned. What do you think? Do you feel my wife would be up to meeting people?"

"Yes, sir. I feel this would be a great opportunity for her to meet people and practise her re-gained interactive skills. She is not getting so tired now, but perhaps an afternoon rest would be advisable. I believe she would, no doubt, be daunted by the idea to a certain extent but it would ultimately be of great benefit to her. When do you plan to have this soirée?"

"Oh, the Saturday after next, that would be (taking out his diary), yes 9th July, if you feel that is not too short a time to prepare. Obviously I will need to take on more staff for the evening but Dinah can arrange that. I will expect you to attend to be on hand in case my wife needs assistance."

"Thank you, sir. I am most honoured.

"Yes, indeed. Hmm, yes, here (and he offered me some money) - go into town and buy something more suitable to wear, not fancy, we don't want to outshine the other ladies, now do we?"

"Thank you again, sir. I'm extremely grateful."

He then took my hand and kissed it gently, "You're welcome."

CHAPTER 5

I'd bought myself a dress, dark blue with a wide lacy collar, set just off the neck line, descending into a 'V' line but not too revealing. It was tight-waisted with buttons down the front to a pointed 'V ending below the waist, where the skirt began, flounced over quite a few petticoats. The sleeves were tight at the top with bows ending the sleeves at the elbows. It felt really strange to wear it. Of course, it needed a corset underneath, which I got Dinah to help me with. I'd parted my hair in the centre, as was the fashion and put into a bun at the back of my head.

I'd helped Mrs Meigh dress. Because of her age, she'd chosen something more subdued, a beige off-the-shoulder dress, again corseted to the 'V' shaped waist, with volumous skirts. From the neckline descended a 5 inch parapet of material all round that covered the upper arms. At centre front the parapet opened to reveal a lank bow of the same material. The sleeves were full length, tight to her wrists. She also carried a long shawl of tartan effect in brown hues, which was positioned round the back of her waist and over her forearms. I'd worked especially on Mrs Meigh's hair, curling her hair at the sides into ringlets. She was feeling nervous but, then again, so was I, so we sang a few ditties together to ease the tension.

The dining room was being prepared by the extra staff with the long table decorated with flowers and candelabra and bowls of fruit, containing everything from apples to exotic figs and dates – a silver service setting with beautifully ornate china plates, and wine, water and fruit glasses for each setting. Dinah had been busy all day in the kitchen preparing loads of dishes and a highly decorated cake for the occasion. I was beginning to wonder how many people would be attending this event but Dinah explained that she liked to give a choice to guests so they could pick and choose what they wanted. This, however, meant that she would be preparing up to three times the number of meals as to guests.

There was also a soup starter and all manner of cheese and biscuits and home-made bread with butter.

Soup	*Cucumber Soup*
Fish	*Baked Dover Sole*
Game or Poultry	*Pheasant Mandarin*
Meat with Mushrooms	*Veal Escalopes*
Vegetable	*Carrots Vichy*
Dessert	*Gooseberry Fool*
Cake	
Cheese and Biscuits	
Fruit	
Savoury	*Angels on Horseback*

I looked at the printed menu and wondered about the

savory section as a final course. "Oh" Dinah exclaimed, "It's all the rage now to 've a savoury course after the dessert. Not everyone will 've it, of course. It's normally served with coffee, to the men, after the ladies have resettled in the music room, leaving the men to smoke and talk at the table."

Little did I know at the time that the millions of people in Staffordshire and the surrounding counties would soon be starving and would have been grateful just for the pickings off the plates. I, for one, would not be able to eat much, what with being trussed up so I could barely breathe, no matter how hungry I felt.

Joseph Weston, the coachman was acting as butler. He was dressed up in a fine, red, pseudo military suit with epaulets and brass buttons. He would also be in charge of serving the wines. John Woods would be caring for the horses and parking carriages. Harriet Jones had been working all day with Dinah preparing the meals with an additional girl. There were other staff laid on to serve and take coats.

John assisted Mrs Meigh into her harness to lower her downstairs. She had her walking stick with her to steady herself. I showed her to an armchair in the dining room and waited with her for the first guests to arrive. Mr Meigh arrived. He was quite resplendent in a double-breasted, flared frock-coat tightly clinching at the waist, over a white waistcoat and tight trousers. His collar was high and upstanding with a frilled necktie tied round and tucked into the waistcoat. His moustache and side-burns had been trimmed. He looked nervous too, pacing up and down and repeatedly looking out of the window.

A carriage soon rolled up the drive and I could see John

assisting a lady to descend. Minutes later Joseph Weston entered the room and announced: Sir Smith-Child, 1st Baronet and Lady Sarah.

Mr Meigh went to shake his hand and bowed to Lady Sarah. He directed them to glasses of wine or fruit juice, which were poured and waiting on the sideboard. He them introduced them to his wife. He introduced me as Jane Paget, physiotherapist, daughter to Mr Paget, lawyer in Lincoln Inn Fields, London, and good friend to him and his wife. I was most bemused by that but, hey ho, whatever kept his boat afloat!

I could see that the Baronet was about 34-35 years old, so quite a bit younger than Job Meigh. He also sported a frock coat and cravat. His fair hair was long, swept to the sides and he also had a moustache and sideburns. Lady Sarah was quite beautiful and wore a stunning dress of white silk with a lace covering. It was an up-to-date off-the shoulder dress, ruched around the bust line with ruched and layered short sleeves. The dress was decorated at the cleavage with a small rosette, which was repeated on the front, either side of the heavily petticoated skirt.

Other guests started arriving, and I heard Joseph Weston announcing one by one as they entered:

Mr William Brownfield,
Thomas and Harriet Peake,
Thomas Sparrow Wilkinson
Joseph Clementson and Martha Clementson
Mr Rose, Magistrate
Mr Ralph Adderley and Rosamond Adderley
Mr Philip Barnes Broade

Richard Edensor Heathcote
Sir Smith-Child, Magistrate

Unfortunately, the gentlemen seemed to outnumber the ladies to some degree but maybe Mr Meigh didn't get the opportunity to mix much with ladies, being in a male-orientated world of business or the gentlemen invited were unattached for some reason.

Each of the ladies, however, came to say hello to Mrs Meigh and I got the chance to introduce myself as Jane Paget, physiotherapist. I didn't feel so bad now being there. Job Meigh had saved my face. I was, to all intense and purposes, an educated person with a position of standing, not just a lowly servant, who had no right to be there, let alone in an evening dress.

When I got the chance, I started to ask Mrs Meigh about the guests. Her speech had improved considerably following our voice exercises, although it was delivered slowly and with more deliberation. "Sir Smith-Child is a Conservative and may well enter into politics at a later date. He married Sarah five years ago, a good marriage, as she is an heiress, daughter of Richard Clarke Hill of Stallington Hall, Stone, Staffordshire." He looked kindly. Mrs Meigh continued, "They have three children. Sir Smith-Child is known to be quite a philanthropist. He's a good man, contributing annually to the Staffordshire Infirmary as well as many other good causes, such as supporting medical institutions in Tunstall. He has high plans for developing Tunstall when he eventually becomes and MP." Lady Sarah, his wife, was wearing a beautiful, flouncing, pale blue ball gown, off the shoulders, as per the fashion, with little puffed sleeves with frills of lace. Her hair was tied back in a bun, parted in the centre, but to which she had attached an artificial flower, which looked quite becoming.

"What about that rather dour-looking man over there." I indicated a thin man, in his 60s, on the far side. He had white, short-cut wavy hair, that I imagined would have been fair in earlier life, and trim grey sideburns. "He looks so sad and I don't think he came with anyone. Is he married?"

"I believe you mean Mr Richard Edensor Heathcote. Well, that's a story in itself. He inherited Longton in 1822, together with a lot of other landed property, on the death of his father. You think he would be made but he's had a terrible life with successive bereavements, legal battles, treacherous servants, wrangles with relatives over property, as well as political disappointments, that led him into such depths of despair that he almost didn't recover."

Just then, the bell rang for people to take their seats for the repast.

"I'll continue with Mr Heathcote's story later on, if I get the chance."

Male guests had been assigned to a female guest to escort into the dining room. Mr Meigh escorted Lady Sarah Smith-Child, being the highest ranking lady. Mrs Meigh was escorted by Mr Thomas Sparrow Wilkinson, being an associate of her husband's. I was escorted by Mr William Brownfield, who was about 30 years old.

I sat next to Mrs Meigh in case she required any help with her meal. I was able to reach over and get any particular offering she required and ensure it was in bite-sized niblets. I didn't want a possible embarrassment caused by Mrs Meigh spilling something when reaching over or actually going without, because she was frightened of spilling something.

First of all, Mr Meigh led a thanksgiving prayer, which everyone around the table concluded with "Amen".

Luckily, Mrs Meigh was able to give me a potted version of the people seated, not that I was going to be able to remember everything:

Mr Philip Barnes Broade, a Magistrate, had the Minerva Pottery works in Park Street, Fenton. He owed four fifths of the Fenton Hall estate, the rest now being owned by Sir Smith-Child, also a stipendiary Magistrate.

Mr William Brownfield owned the Wood and Brownfield pottery. He was a Whig and member of the Bethseda New Connection.

Thomas Sparrow Wilkinson was a potter at A J Wilkinson. His family was listed in Burke's Peerage. He looked in his early 30s.

Thomas Peake was famous for creating blue tiles and bricks at Peakes Tunstall. He and his wife Harriet, had a 5-year-old son, John Nash Peake. Harriet wore a light grey dress, off the shoulders and decorated around the bust area with ruched light blue lace. This same light blue lace covered the skirt. It looked very expensive.

Joseph Clementson owned the Phoenix Works at Shelton and was another member of the Bethseda New Connection. His wife, Martha was wearing a dark blue tartan patterned dress with multiple pleats coming off from the waist. It looked fairly heavy for a summer's day but, on further inspection, proved to be a light cotton. The dress had a wide band of the same tartan material passing from the waist, over the shoulders and top of the arms, around the neck and back to the waist, and a 'V' neck. Mrs Meigh called it a pelerine.

Mr Rose was a Magistrate. He'd come on his own but looked extremely smart, straight-backed, slim, with a commanding manner.

Mr Ralph Adderley was a landowner, having Coton Hall, Barlaston Hall and Tunstall Hall. His family was also listed in Burke's Peerage. He looked about 60. He was a bit portly with curly brown hair, brushed back over a high white collar. He wore a frock coat and round glasses. Rosamond, his wife wore a burgundy red satin dress, the material of which, I had noticed earlier, while standing, bore a vertical stripe pattern, alternate burgundy stripe with a light grey stripe from waist to hem. From the waist up, the dress resembled a tunic with woven button loops up to a black lace round collar.

Then back to Richard Edensor Heathcote, whom Mrs Meigh advised had been an MP at one point until he became ill.

The conversation started off as complimentary about the meal and general chit-chat about the gorgeous weather and who had been to visit whom. Mr Heathcote mentioned that he had given up his residency at Longton and had leased it out.

Mr Heathcote turned out to be a quite riveting speaker, getting the attention of his audience around the table.

Sir Smith-Child began asking Mr Heathcote if there were any further news on bringing the railway to the Pottery towns.

"Well, for those who are interested and do not know, some time ago now, actually January 13th, 1835, I chaired a meeting at the Swan Hotel, Hanley, of leading citizens, some of whom are here now, who were interested in bringing the railway here. It would have been a valiant enterprise, another way of transporting our products, pottery and coal, as well as copper and agricultural produce, to interested buyers throughout Britain as both the Trent and Mersey are slow means of transporting goods. I had been in talks with George Stephenson, who drew up a plan for a railway from Norton Bridge on the Grand Junction Railway, to Harecastle. There would be one branch line through Newcastle to the Apedale canal wharf on Liverpool Road, Apedale being my residential seat. However, one rival scheme after another has been put forward over the years and, unfortunately, I have to submit that Stephenson's plan has been prevented, at this point in time, from parliamentary approval."

Someone else added, "Yes, I believe you suffered some ill health, which unfortunately led to your resigning your parliamentary seat in 1836. I trust that you are better now."

"Yes, thank you; however, I do not get out and about as much and have cut down on personal engagements, preferring to stay at Apedale. I have also suffered some personal losses - that of my elder son George on 4th January 1835, followed tragically by my second son, William on 8th April 1838, at the tender age of eight."

There were murmurs of condolences around the table.

Mr Heathcote continued, "I do have other interests though. Something that has arisen on my own doorstep – iron-making! I successfully persuaded Thomas Firmstone to give up his Apedale lease, an amicable arrangement, as Firmstone was more interested in Leycett coal and iron-working, and the prospects of an easy rail link to Madeley and the Grand Junction line. So, I have been busy making improvements and increased output, confidently expecting the railway to arrive in the valley in a year or two. There were already two blast furnaces in existence and I am now pleased to say that I have implemented a third, which is now up and running."

Congratulations were hoisted on Mr Heathcote for his valiant efforts.

"I apologise for the details, as I am sure you ladies will not be interested, so please talk amongst yourselves, but I will continue to anyone willing to listen. I have increased coal and ironstone supplies, improving Watermills Colliery, and installed a steam engine to replace the water-powered pumping and winding gear, where, you may be interested to know, the name Watermills originated."

Congratulations went up again at the table. However, I overheard Mr Brownfield whispering to Mr Meigh that he hoped Mr Heathcote would not fall foul of the lowering iron prices causing severe competition in the iron trade. The market was not good at the moment and there didn't look to be any let up in the near future. Mr Meigh agreed, adding, "the situation may well lead to a down-turn in manufacture and laying-off of workers. If the introduction of the railway to the area is not agreed soon, I can see Mr Heathcote getting into some trouble."

Mr Heathcote continued, "You will be able to congratulate me further when I tell you my other more personal news." There was an excited whispering around the table. "Yes, I wish to add that I became a father again in November 1840. The little lad, as he is indeed a boy, we have named Michael, and he is now toddling around – quite a mischievous, inquisitive boy but quite adorable – a boon to my, soon to be, old age.

This news was greeted with applause and some of the gentlemen got up and clapped Mr Heathcote on the back, which caused a round of coughing on his part, followed by apologies from the gentlemen, having forgotten that Mr Heathcote had been ill.

I noticed that not many people were actually drinking the wine. Mrs Meigh explained that most of the men, like her husband were New Connection Methodists, connected to Bethseda Chapel in Hanley. Methodists quite often abstained from alcohol but could imbibe, if usage was controlled and did not lead to alcohol abuse.

Just then, Mrs Meigh was interrupted by Mr William Brownfield, who sat opposite us. "Oh, you're talking about Bethseda Chapel. A fine place but not, by far, big enough for the congregation we have built up. The congregation is twice as large as that of St John's. It's frequented and supported by quite a few of the leading pottery manufacturers, such as myself, the Ridgway family, whose factory stands just over the road from the chapel, and Michael Huntbach."

'Huntbach' rang a bell to me. Yes, Huntbach Street, where I'd go down to park the car when driving to Hanley. There were quite a few roads named after these entrepreneurs of the pottery and mining industries, including Meigh Street – there being two, one in Hanley and one in Werrington, close by Ash Hall.

Mr Brownfield continued, that our host today, and of course Mrs Meigh, are prominent members and supporters plus, indeed, is Joseph Clementson, seated to your right." Of course, I thought, another street dedicated to the memory of a potter, although not actually a street, but a car park, off Clough Street in Hanley - Clementson Car Park. Maybe, I thought, there might have been a Clementson Street at one time.

"So, Mr Brownfield," I said, "could you please advise more about the New Connection Methodists. I haven't heard of them, not coming from the region. Are they a break-away sect?"

"Yes, certainly, my dear." Mr Brownfield replied, "I thank you for your interest. I'll try to put this as succinctly as possible. A group broke away from the main Methodist body over questions of church government and discipline. This group became known as the 'Kilhamites' or 'Methodist New Connexion'. Alexander Kilham denounced the Methodists for giving too much power to church ministers, at the expense of the laity. We have had some success in the Pottery towns, but particularly in the area around Hanley and Shelton.

This may have been due to the influence of the pottery manufacturers, mainly William Smith, Job Meigh, the first, and George and Job Ridgway, whom I mentioned before. Henry Wedgwood called him, 'one of the most remarkable men Staffordshire ever gave birth to'. Ridgway was one of the founding fathers and leading figures at Bethesda Chapel in Albion Street, Hanley. Because the congregation was expanding and the chapel was still too small, Ridgway and his associates demolished it and replaced it with the present chapel in 1820. This current chapel seats 3,000 people and became known as "The Cathedral of the Potteries." To think this started just from meetings in a house of one of its prominent members. They then acquired a coach-house at the corner of the street where the chapel is. The original chapel housed just 600 people, but then expanded to 1000. Of course, with all of these prominent people involved, Bethesda Chapel is not just a place of worship but has developed as a meeting place for discussions on everything affecting the people of Hanley and the area and a getting together of philanthropists to contribute to growth and well-being.

Mr Clementson had become interested in the conversation since hearing his name mentioned. He now introduced himself, stating his connection to Bethseda Chapel and stating that his youngest daughter, Lucy, was sweet on someone training to be a minister there.

He had a strange accent, not quite local, a twinge of somewhere else. "Excuse me if I appear cheeky, Mr Clementson, but accents fascinate me and I can hear you are not from this area originally. May I ask your origins?"

"Nooh problem, lass. I'm originally from Carrigill in Cumberland."

Cumberland, I thought to myself, mmm Oh, yes, Cumbria – the country name was changed back in the 1960s or around then. Of course, saying back in the 1960s, I meant, Cumberland will be changed to Cumbria in the future.

Mr Clementson continued that he came to the Potteries in 1811. He looked about 50, so he must have been around 17 or so. He worked first as a collier. In 1820 he apprenticed himself to J. and W. Ridgway, and by 1832 was able to set up his own business at the Phoenix Works, Shelton, in partnership with Jonah Read.

The partnership ended in 1839 and Mr Clementson

continued on his own. He carried on speaking, saying that he had plans to enlarge the works as he was doing so well. Mr Clementson also added that he'd managed to do a bit of travelling while in partnership with Jonah Read and had got to Canada. There he'd laid the foundation for a successful export business to Canada. He added that he had four sons, to whom he hoped to leave the business when he retired. He also added, with a big beaming smile, that his wife had now borne him eight children in all.

The meal finally came to a conclusion and the ladies migrated to the music room, leaving the gentlemen to their cigars, and Angels on Horseback, if they so desired.

I assisted Mrs Meigh into the music room and to a comfy armchair. The room was quite a large room, beautifully decorated with a flower-pattern wallpaper, a grand, ornate fireplace and two chandeliers hanging each end of the room. A grand piano had been placed in one of the large bay windows, with ornate heavy, embroidered curtains and pelmets at the windows. Settees and armchairs and other chairs had been arranged around the walls, leaving a large, uncarpeted area in the centre. Plants in exquisitely painted china pots were placed at intervals throughout the room on tables, also used for drink stands. I had to think back, as this room was unrecognisable to me. I had got myself so embroiled into the 19th century that I was beginning to lose sight of the 21st century, but it must be the entertainments room - games room, come exercise room, come TV room. The ornate fireplace had been taken out and this was where a screen would descend to show films. There was modern lighting in place of the chandeliers and blackout blinds at the windows. I think there was an upright piano on one wall.

A call went up for someone to give a tune on the piano or sing a song.

Martha Clementson said she would play, if one of the gentlemen could accompany her. A servant was sent to the other room to request the attendance of Mr Clementson, who agreed to sing. Of course her husband was the best choice and Martha accompanied him to 'Come into the Garden Maud' – a tune popular at time, written by Alfred Lord Tennyson.

> *Come into the garden, Maud,*
> *For the black bat, night, has flown.*
> *Come into the garden, Maud,*
> *I am here at the gate alone;*
> *And the woodbine spices are wafted abroad,*
> *And the musk of the rose is blown.*

This was quite a long song and everyone seemed to be appreciative. I approached Mrs Meigh to continue with her story about Mr Heathcote as he was out of earshot.

"Oh yes, mmm. It's quite an intriguing story. He's had a lot of sadness in his life. His twelve-year old daughter died in '24 after a short illness. He started building his own mansion in Apedale building partly on the foundations of the medieval hall. However, before the first stage of this new building was ready for occupation, his second wife, Lady Elizabeth, died at Longton in August '25 at the age of 44. During the next year he was in great despair and on the verge of giving up all, when an escape offered itself.

Political friends persuaded him to take the Coventry seat in Parliament. Here's where the intrigue comes in. He was only 46, and a widower, so he decided to take a third wife but in circumstances which made the outside world almost completely disregard both the marriage and the lady concerned. The family tree shows only '3rd wife – Susanna Cooper. The rumours are that he had originally added 'daughter of Mr John Cooper of Jefference Hayes', but then withdrew this comment."

Mrs Meigh had paused and the song continued in the background.

> I said to the rose, 'The brief night goes
> In babble and revel and wine.
> O young lord-lover, what sighs are those,
> For one that will never be thine?
> But mine, but mine,' so I sware to the rose,
> 'For ever and ever, mine.'

Mrs Meigh continued again. "No date was given in either private or published notes for the third wedding – nothing at all about this third marriage in the Peerage Registry. However, they both seem to have been happy and he has been with Susan longer than either of his first wives, but there appears to have been a conspiracy to totally ignore Susan. For a start, it appears that Susan's father was probably a farm labourer at Jefference Hayes, Audley, and the Heathcotes had opposed this liaison with a young lady of no pedigree or social standing and there seems to have been a conspiracy to totally ignore Susan. Richard Heathcote was obviously besmitten by this female though and resented the opposition from other people to their 'association', stating that he married her because he was lonely and he was infatuated with her. I mean, I can understand him being lonely, but you don't associate yourself with a farm girl, 20 years your junior, and marry her, of all things, just because you're lonely. Also, his second wife was only buried six months earlier. Just not the done thing! There was talk that she, in all probability, had been employed by his second wife as a maid or children's nurse. Plus, to make matters worse, no-one one we know actually attended this wedding. Did it actually take place? Has he been living in sin all of this time, and fathering three…. (quietly) bastards? He won't say where the wedding took place and when. Susan has produced three sons to Richard but misfortune struck again and the first two died very young. Also, to add to rumours, there's a tomb for the second son of that union, erected in Audley churchyard in 1838, but no family name appears on it, only a monogrammed 'H' plus something like 'In memory of two beloved children, by their deeply afflicted but entirely resigned parents.' All he does say is that Susan is shy and retiring and is unable to move in the same social circles as himself. I was quite surprised that Job invited him this evening and that is probably why there so few ladies have attended, especially when you take into account that most of the people here are religious, upstanding members of the community. Oh well, as long as he's kept her away, that's all that matters. Job probably wanted to find out what he'd been doing commercially, not having heard from him for some time."

Just at that time, the duet was coming to an end with the last two verses.

There has fallen a splendid tear
From the passion-flower at the gate.
She is coming, my dove, my dear;
She is coming, my life, my fate;

The red rose cries, 'She is near, she is near;'
And the white rose weeps, 'She is late;'
The larkspur listens, 'I hear, I hear;'
And the lily whispers, 'I wait.'

She is coming, my own, my sweet,
Were it ever so airy a treat,
My heart would hear her and beat,
Were it earth in an earthy bed;

My dust would hear her and beat,
Had I lain for a century dead;
Would start and tremble under her feet,
And blossom in purple and red.

Mr Meigh was saying that that was a bit sad and that we needed something jolly to entertain us all. We need some dancing. Can someone give us a waltz on the piano? It will have to be a gentleman to allow our charming Mrs Clementson to dance, if she will. Thomas Peake came forward. "Honoured sir," and started playing something from Johann Strauss. Immediately people started re-arranging the furniture to make more room for dancing then got themselves into couples for the waltz. There was a lot of gaity and laughter amongst the ladies.

"Come, Jane." Came Mr Meigh's voice from behind

me, "We cannot have you sitting this one out. I insist you join me in a waltz."

"I am honoured, sir, but I'm afraid I am not a good dancer. You would be better choosing someone else."

"I'll hear nothing of the sort, come Jane." and he took me by the arm and led me into the waltz. As it happens, he was a very good lead, so I didn't manage to step on his toes, even in the multi-pettitcoated dress and not being able to see where my feet were going.

At last things calmed down a bit and a couple of the men started talking together. I feigned tiredness after the exercise and needed to sit down. Mr Sparrow Wilkinson continued playing and the ladies were taking turns accompanying him in song.

Mrs Meigh had her back to me, talking with the ladies who were not singing. I don't think she meant to have her back to me but I got the distinct impression that the other ladies did not know quite what to think of me and were asking questions but did not want to approach me directly. Probably they couldn't work out whether I was working for myself or was a servant to the Meighs. Obviously, they must be thinking that, if I were a servant, I had no reason being there and should be treated as persona non grata. Oh well, too bad, I didn't belong in their age anyway. Let them get on with their silly class distinctions.

Just then, one of the ladies announced that we would all be playing a game. Oh, what fun, I thought – not – what have they got in store for me now. Anyway, at least they weren't talking about me - that was just my own imagination and insecurity.

So, what they had in store for everyone was something

that turned out to be something like, if 'Simon Says' and 'Musical Chairs' had an illegitimate love child, this game would be it. It was just called 'Change Seats'. As soon as it was announced, people started moving plants and breakable objects out of the room and started collecting dining chairs. Obviously, they knew what to expect. As I was to find out, one person is 'it'. They stand in the middle while everyone else sits around them in a circle of chairs. The player in the middle asked someone in the circle, "Do you have a daughter?". The person has the option to say "No", which forces the people adjacent to them to run around the circle and try to grab a new seat, or they can say, "Yes, except those who wear.... (brown, blue, etc.), at which point, anyone who meets the criteria has to scramble for a chair. The person in the middle will almost always get a chair because they are so much closer, so the one left over player takes their spot. There didn't appear to be a way of winning this game. I don't think that was the ethic of the game, just to have a bit of fun. So, there was nothing like musical chairs, where one chair is taken away at a time before the music stops. I wasn't going to tell them that one as it was chaos now with people falling over themselves to get to a chair. No wonder anything breakable had to be cleared from the room first of all. Anyway, this frolicking finally came to an end when everyone had had a go and I managed to find myself a seat to relax. Someone started playing the piano again, but a little bit of light classical.

So, I found myself listening into the conversation between Mr Brownfield and Thomas Sparrow Wilkinson, who were standing close by. They were talking politics. "… The working classes have now proved themselves unworthy of that extension of the Suffrage for which they contended in May with their People's Charter presented to Parliament." This was Thomas Sparrow Wilkinson speaking. "It is now established beyond all doubt, that Universal Suffrage in reality means nothing else but universal pillage. What the working classes understand by political power, is just the means of putting their hands in their neighbour's. It was their belief that the Reform Bill would give them that power, which was the main cause of the enthusiasm in its favour and the disgust of the failure of these hopes, the principal reason of the present clamour for an extension of the Suffrage. The Tories feel that this Chartist movement is directed less against the privileged condition of society, than against capitalists in general. The movement is, in fact, an insurrection which is expressly directed against the middle classes. A change in the system of government is demanded by the Chartists not for the purpose of receiving more power and privileges but, as far as their aim permits any definition, for the purpose of producing a hitherto non-existent condition of society, in which wage, labour and capital do not exist at all."

Mr Brownfield's retort was, "However, sir, I must add that the people were never as determined as at the present moment by every constitutional means to obtain the franchise. When they see their interests disregarded, and their feelings insulted, and when they have no hope of better times or better treatment, unless they work out their own redress, when the Tories offer them more words, and endeavour to stop their cravings by the delusive promises of a Queen's speech – when they tell them that 'they feel extremely for the distress of the manufacturing districts, which they have borne with exemplary patience and fortitude' but offer them no remedy beyond your compassion. What can you expect but that they should make their way to Parliament and, as the Tories will do nothing for them, endeavour to do something for themselves? I, and the Whigs, feel that nothing but a radical change in the constitution of the House would ever give people what they should have a right to."

"Quite right." Replied Thomas Sparrow-Wilkinson. "Sir James Graham, the Home Secretary, accepted the principles of the petition and agreed that distress was a real problem, but still does not think that Chartism is the answer. It was felt, when the petition was presented, that to hear the petitioners would raise false hope. The Government believes that the solution rests in sound economic policies such as free trade, not in constitutional reforms."

"Yes," Mr Brownfield replied, "it seems that the Whig leader, Lord Russell, also thought that hearing the petition was undesirable and not in the national interest. He expressed his 'abhorrence of the doctrine set forth in the petition'. He believes that, if the present working class were enfranchised then violent Chartists would be elected and the threat to property is obvious. He also sees a potential threat to the stability of government if the moderates lose control of parliament."

Thomas Sparrow-Wilkinson continued, "The Prime Minister, Sir Robert Peel, was also against the Charter and actually opposed hearing the Chartists, for reasons similar to Graham's. Peel based his attack on the belief in further socio-economic reform as the solution to the problem of distress. As you know, Mr Thomas Duncombe, MP for

Finsbury, presented the Charter. Mr Thomas Babington Macaulay gave a speech in Parliament in opposition of the petition stating that, what the petitioners demanded was that the House forthwith passed what is called the people's Charter into a law, without alteration, diminution, or addition! This petition did not tell the House to inquire - it told them **not** to do so, and directed the House to pass a certain law **word for word**, and to pass it **without the smallest delay**. He then went on to state there are six points of the Charter, one of which he had voted for, one of which he did not approve and others which he could go some way to meet. For your information, or to remind you, the six points in the Charter were:

A ballot box for voting

Each Member of Parliament represent the same number of electors

All men to be eligible for Parliament without a proper qualification

Annual elections for Parliament

Payment to MPs

Suffrage for all able-minded men 21 years of age."

Oh, I thought to myself. That's what the Charter was all about. It was presented to Parliament in May, citing these six points, for consideration – or not even that - for immediate passage through Parliament, without consideration - and was seemingly refused. Hopefully, Mr Sparrow-Wilkinson was going to explain why.

Mr Sparrow-Wilkinson continued, "There was, in fact, only one of the six points on which he was diametrically opposed, but that happened to be infinitely the most important of the six…. Gentlemen, I have a parliamentary paper here that explains Mr Macauley's objections. I shall try to precis this paper, if no-one has any objection, as it is quite protracted and Macauley has a tendency to be rather explicit in his views, with quite descriptive dialogue, that some might categorise as long-winded, although I would say he certainly has a gift for expressing himself eloquently."

There were eager ears for Mr Thomas Sparrow-Wilkinson to continue as there had been no full explanation of why the Charter had been rejected.

"Thank you gentlemen. I will, therefore, continue, but I probably should advise you to take seats, as this objection goes into great detail and is rather long in explanation." The interested gentlemen, gathered round and seated themselves.

"One of the six points was the ballot, which Mr Macauley had no objection to. Another point was the abolition of the pecuniary qualification for members of the House, which Mr Macauley cordially agreed with. He stated it is surely absurd to admit the representatives of Edinburgh and Glasgow without any qualification and, at the same time, to require the representative of Finsbury or Marylebone to possess a qualification or the semblance of one. Mr Macauley believed that the qualification is no security at all and should not be required from anyone."

Here Mr Thomas Sparrow-Wilkinson read: "It is no part of the old constitution of the realm. It was first established in the reign of Anne. It was established by a bad parliament for a bad purpose. It was, in fact, part of a course of legislation which, if it had not been happily interrupted, would have ended in the repeal of the Toleration Act and of the Act of Settlement."

Mr Thomas Sparrow-Wilkinson continued, "The Chartists demanded annual parliaments and payment to representatives of the people. Here Mr Macauley was willing to come to some compromise. He differed from them also as to dividing the country into electoral districts. He, however, did not consider these matters as vital, as he said the kingdom could prosper even though the members of the House were to receive salaries and the present boundaries of counties and boroughs were superseded by new lines of demarcation.

What Mr Macauley thought the essence of the Charter was though, was universal suffrage. He felt that, 'if you withhold that, it matters not very much what else you grant. If you grant that, it matters not at all what else you withhold. If you grant that, the country is lost!'

Mr Macauley went on to say that he is 'bound by no tie to oppose any reform, which he thinks likely to promote the public good'. He did not go so far as to say he did not 'quite agree with those who think that they have proved the People's Charter to be absurd, when they have proved that it is incompatible with the existence of the throne and of the peerage'. He continued, 'I cannot consider either monarchy or aristocracy as the ends of government. They are only means. Nations have flourished without hereditary sovereigns or assemblies of nobles; and, though I should be very sorry to see England a republic, I do not doubt that she might, as a republic, enjoy prosperity, tranquillity, and high consideration'. Mr Macauley stated, in his own words, that he views universal suffrage with dread and aversion but stated that this might be greatly diminished if he could believe that the worst effect it would produce would be to give us an elective first magistrate and a senate instead of a Queen and a House of Peers. His firm conviction is that, in our country, universal suffrage is incompatible, not with this or that form of government, but with all forms of government, and with everything for the sake of which forms of government exist; that it is incompatible with property, and that it is consequently incompatible with civilisation.'."

There were exclamations from those listening of, "That's harsh". "Surely not", "He doesn't mince his words", "He must know what he's saying", "We are royalists, this Charter must be banned." "Long live Her Majesty, Queen Victoria".

Mr Thomas Sparrow-Wilkinson continued, part reading, part précising the document. "I will try to be more precise with Mr Macauley's views on why the working classes should not be given the vote, if you could bear with me. Mr Macauley felt, at the time the Charter was presented in May that, 'giving supreme power to a class that would not be likely to respect the institution of property, through ignorance, would lead to plunder of every man in the kingdom who has a good roof over his head. The petitioners complain they are enormously taxed to pay the interest of the national debt, expended in the Napoleonic wars and other expensive wars for the suppression of liberty. They meant that the present generation should not be bound to pay debt incurred by our rulers in past times. They wish monopoly of land and machinery and ownership to cease. All canal property and railway property in the kingdom to be confiscated. They wish to ruin anyone earning £100 a year. Imagine a well-meaning, laborious mechanic, fondly attached to his wife and children. Bad times come. He sees the wife whom he loves grow thinner and paler every day. His little ones cry for bread, and he has none to give them. Then come the professional agitators, the tempters, and tell him that there is enough and more than enough for everybody, and that he has too little, only because landed gentlemen, fundholders, bankers, manufacturers, railway proprietors, shopkeepers have too much. Is it strange that the poor man should be deluded, and should eagerly sign such a petition as this? Our honest working man has not received such an education as enables him to understand that the utmost distress that he has ever known is prosperity when compared with the distress which he would have to endure if there were a single month of general anarchy and plunder. What we are asked to do is to give universal suffrage before there is universal education.'

Mr Macauley goes on to say that the Chartists expect the Government to support the people. They suppose the Government has an inexhaustible storehouse of money to use to improve workers lives but they refuse to do so out of mere hardheartedness. This Charter would give the people now less than absolute and irresistible power. 'The distress would be far greater than before. The fences which now protect property would all have been broken through, levelled, swept away. The new proprietors would have no title to show to anything that they held. There would be many millions of human beings, crowded in a narrow space, deprived of all those resources which alone had made it possible for them to exist in so narrow a space; trade gone; manufactures gone; credit gone. What could they do but fight for the mere sustenance of nature, and tear each other to pieces till famine, and pestilence following in the train of famine, came to turn the terrible commotion into a more terrible repose?'

This would lead to military rule but our nation would never again see the likes again of the liberty, wealth, knowledge and arts we have produced. All those nations which envy our greatness would insult our downfall."

For me, that speech was incomprehensible and nonsensical. Everyone has the vote now – universal suffrage, and we still have a monarchy. But, what he was saying was that the monarchy could not survive if the people in general had the vote. He was saying that, if the uneducated people had the vote, they would disperse the coffers and land, machinery, property, would be owned by the people and it would mean the end of any government and was incompatible with people owning property.

Trying to delve into my vague memories of various history programmes on TV and books I'd read, I recalled that British politicians faced a crisis when the overthrow of the centuries-old Romanov monarchy and the Russian nobility in March 1917 and the subsequent revolution of workers and soldiers in November, raised the possibility of a similar socialist revolution in Britain. The Home Secretary, at the time, in some act or other of 1918 – something like 'The Representation of the People Act' basically stated that war, by all classes, had brought the nation together, making it impossible there should ever be a revival of the old class feeling, which was responsible for exclusion of so many of the population from voting. This was the act that abolished practically all property qualifications for men and gave voting rights to women over 30, as long as they met minimum property qualifications. Actually, women who owned property had got the vote decades before, but now, those who didn't own property were accepted due, so it was said, to their contribution in the First World War. There was another reason, however, why women couldn't get voting rights, unless they were over 30, and this was to ensure all men over the age of 21, had been given these rights first, plus it was thought inappropriate to introduce women as the majority voters, especially after the hardships men had faced in the trenches, and the decimation of the male population in the war, so they cut down the possible numbers of women voters by adding this stipulation that they had to be over 30. Women over 21 didn't get the vote until 1928.

My attention had wandered for a while but, I now returned to Sir Smith-Child's commenting. "There's just another bit here at the bottom. These objections to the Charter presented in May, notwithstanding, have not prevented the Chartists holding regular meetings in the town, and Manchester and I do believe, without governmental changes being put into force within the near future, we are more than likely going to get more than marches and demonstrations. (He tweaked his moustache). There is great distress. The working people need food, clothing, good hours of work, good beds and good substantial furniture for every man, woman and child, who will do a fair day's work (while speaking, he was banging his fist on the back of a chair to emphasise each point mentioned). When trade is poor, people are laid off but there is no poor relief anymore, following the Poor Law Act of '34. All there is now, for these people laid off, are the workhouses. (He tweaked his moustache again, rather nervously). New trade policies need to be put in place, foreign trade. I have not known, as yet, a case of plunder in the town, though thousands have marched through its streets to meetings in various places. What they want is a voice in making the laws they are called to obey. They believe that taxation without presentation is tyranny and ought to be resisted. They want fewer working hours, especially for children. They want education, co-operation, civil and religious liberty; plus, I believe there should be medical institutions set up for the health of the workers. (Again he banged his fist on the back of the chair, to emphasise his points). Illness is rife in the town and, if a person cannot work through ill health, they cannot earn. Too many are passing through the doors of these so-called workhouses, through illness and starvation."

Joseph Clementson, who had been within earshot, interjected. "At least Peel is an improvement on that Whig, Lorrd Melbourne. Melbourne was against the '32 Reform Act and, no wonder. He, naturally, wanted to keep the status quo, being one of the aristocrats of this nation, hmmm begging your pardon to those of the aristocracy here present. As I was saying, Melbourne was against the '32 Reform Act, even though the Reform Act did put an end to rotten burroughs, But, of course, it re-distributed poower away from the landed aristocracy to the urban middle classes and, in any case, it did not improve the condition of the people. Hoowever, he did reluctantly agree that it was necessary to forestall the threat of revolution. Of course, he later opposed the repeal of these dreaded Corn Laws that impose steep import duties, and making it tooo expensive to import grain from abroad, even when food supplies are short. We all know that the King tried to oust him from office because of his policies."

Mr. Barnes Broade joined the conversation. "I, for one, am against repeal of the Corn Laws. I believe, and I am backed by the majority of Conservatives in this country, that this would lead to an influx of cheap, foreign corn, and I believe would ruin farmers and cause unemployment in the countryside. Peel wants to bring in free trade and he wants to bring in an income tax - tax us landowners to the hilt. We oppose Peel all the way on this.

I then got a tap on the shoulder and turned to see Mrs Meigh. "Are you getting bored, dear, with all this political talk?"

"Somewhat," I replied, "though more confused. I'm not really into politics and their machinations. They are now talking about Lord Melbourne and Prime Minister Pitt."

"Oh, I've got an interesting story about Melbourne. He was a character – he treated it all as a bit of a game, so didn't really do anything to help anyone, but he had a following. I suppose you know William IV dismissed him as Prime Minister?"

I agreed, as I'd just heard this.

"Yes, well, the King didn't like his policies. This was a strong step for the King to take, to go against his government in this way. Well, Lord Grey resigned in July '34 and the King was forced to appoint another Whig to replace him, as the Tories were not strong enough to support a government. He angered the King so dreadfully with the Whigs' reforming ways, that the King dismissed Melbourne in November. He then gave the Tories, under Robert Peel, a chance to form a government but, unfortunately, he was not able to get a majority in the next general election, which, I believe, was January 1835. So, the Whigs were in power again under Melbourne – that is, until last year when Melbourne's government fell and he resigned. Peel was then offered the post in August…. Have you managed to see either of them while you've been in London? Peel is so handsome, don't you think?"

"Sorry, Mrs Meigh, I have not had the opportunity to go to Westminster, but," I added to give some credence, "I have obviously seen their pictures in the newspapers." (I lied – I'd no idea what they looked like!)

"Anyway", Mrs Meigh continued, "I said I had some gossip about Lord Melbourne, listen closely." I leant closer. "It seems our Lord Melbourne liked to pinch and smack Aristocratic ladies' bottoms when at Court, and it seems some of them liked it. Well, men will be men. As I said, he's quite a character. However, he did get himself into a bit of trouble with some orphan girls taken into his household as objects of charity – it seems he liked to whip these girls. He probably thought he could get away with it, they being only charity orphans and all that, but it seems one of them complained and an investigation was opened. He's probably had to pay a pittance to the girl, so no problem there – and it was all a bit of fun. I'm sure the girls came to no harm."

I could not believe what Mrs Meigh had said – 'whipping girls was a bit of fun.' So, that was what the aristocracy was like in the 19th Century – anything they could get away with, have a laugh and pay them off.

"Anyway, dear, I haven't finished. It seems he also got

himself involved in a sex scandal. This time he was the victim of attempted blackmail from the husband of a close friend, society beauty and author, Caroline Norton. The husband demanded £1,400 and, when he was turned down, he accused Melbourne of having an affair with his wife. Well, this scandal would be enough to derail any major politician and if it wasn't Lord Melbourne and the measure of respect his contemporaries held for his integrity, he would have been out. As it was, the King and the Duke of Wellington urged him to stay on as Prime Minister! All's well that ends well, Norton failed in court and Melbourne was vindicated.

I also have a bit of gossip about Melbourne and the young Queen Victoria. She was barely eighteen when she came to the throne in June '37 – only just breaking free from the domineering influence of her mother, the Duchess of Kent and her mother's advisor, Sir John Conroy. Melbourne, as her Prime Minister, took on the job of training her in the art of politics and it seems the two became friends. Melbourne was given a private apartment at Windsor Castle and he spent four to five hours a day visiting. There were rumours circulating for a time that Victoria would marry Melbourne, even though he was 40 years her senior, but nothing came of them. Then, of course, Albert came on the scene."

Just then, Job Meigh appeared. "May I accompany you in a dance, Jane? You have been sitting for some time. You must be well refreshed now?"

"Thank you, sir, but would you not like to ask your wife to dance?"

"Oh no, Jane, I am simply not up to it." Mrs Meigh replied, "Even after your strenuous exercise regime, I don't think my legs are up to a hop and skip. Please take my husband's arm."

"Oh well, thank you, sir."

I noticed when Mrs Meigh spoke that she barely sent a glance towards her husband. I thought this strange, as I had hoped, and it was proving me right, that the soirée would bring her out of herself, getting her to interact with people and away from her own thoughts of her ill health. She'd been laughing but, as soon as her husband appeared, the smile faded. Maybe, I thought, she did not appreciate his asking me to dance, or maybe just the thought that she was not able, physically, to dance with him had upset her. I had been aware, for some time, that Mr Meigh had not attended any exercise sessions I had held in her room and had not seemed to have any interest in knowing, to any extent, the exercises involved. I took this that, probably, he was just too busy, with his mind on business matters of greater importance. Then again, during the time I had been working there, Mrs Meigh had not particularly spoken of her husband, unless directly asked. However, Mr Meigh had arranged this soirée for his wife, so was obviously thinking of her mental well-being, not just her physical well-being. I believe he had hoped that this evening would bring her out of herself and would bring them closer....... but then again, neither of them had shown any interest in talking to each other this evening, which seemed extremely strange. There must be something more between them than just Mrs Meigh's accident.... as great strides had been made in her physical improvement something that went deeper and, obviously, this evening's get-together was not working for the two of them.

Was this obvious falling out between the two of them, something I had been sent back into the past to correct? I didn't think so. I didn't see myself as that 'Quantum Leap' character, from that old TV programme, where he goes back into the past, appearing as different characters, trying to prevent unfortunate things happening. In any case, this falling out between them was long before I came on the scene so, if I had been sent back to sort out the problem, I'd been sent back too late. I had to find out who the figure was I had seen running away from the nursing home. I'm sure he had some bearing on why I was here but I'd no idea who he was. All I saw was the back of a man, in the dark, running away. I couldn't even work out if he was fair- or dark-haired.

Mr Meigh went to speak to the pianist and the next moment a rousing Galop struck up.

Mr Meigh held me as for a waltz. "I don't know how to dance to this" I whispered.

"Don't worry, I'll whisper the steps to you. It's only a laugh anyway. We'll have fun. Right, slide your feet one to the other in a sort of fast waltz." He danced me round the room.

"Then a jump on alternate feet, like so". The he twirled me round the room again at a fast tempo, then a sort of hand-in-hand walk, then a fast waltz and a return hand-in-hand walk.

He was right, I finally got the hang of it, and it was fun. Others had joined us on the floor, too, all going at some speed around in a circle, sliding, jumping and walking.

"I need to sit down, Mr Meigh, that was fun but, oh, exhausting, but thank you for asking me. You're right, Mrs Meigh could never have undertaken such a dance."

"You're very welcome."

I sat down again. This time in earshot of Mr Adderley and Mr Thomas Peake. "Business has been rather slack lately." Said Mr Peake, "I'm not happy with having to put off some of my workers since the Poor Law was revised in '34 and the workhouses were introduced. It didn't seem to matter so much until recently, as productivity has been good up until now."

"Yes, Mr Adderley, before the workers had the poor relief, don't you know, to tide them over until we could take them back again in better times, but that has gone by the way."

Mr Heathcote joined the conversation, - he'd obviously only picked up on what Mr Peake had been saying. "Yes, if the railway had been brought here, we would have been able to make use of it in transporting our wares, by train, to more destinations, and open up more trade. As it happens, I feel trade is stagnating, what with the additional tariffs put on exports, which has been putting off buyers from foreign climes. I feel the government is not assisting merchants in our endeavours."

"We, the merchants, can survive," added Mr Peake, "but before you entered the conversation, Mr Heathcote, we were discussing the misfortunes of the workers, should we have to lay them off. But, I can see no other way. Yes, they can pawn what little possessions they have to get by, but what if this down-turn is extended? We cannot pay the workers for no production, we would soon be out of business."

"These workhouses seem to pass muster if they are not overstretched," said Mr Adderley, "although they split families up, males on one side and females the other, which does not seem correct in the eyes of the church. It is written in the marriage vows that, when man and woman are united in the eyes of God, no man should put asunder, which goes against the grain somewhat."

"Some would see that as a good thing," said Mr Heathcote, "Some would say, that if these folk cannot feed their families, they shouldn't have so many children, and the best thing would be to keep them apart, so no more are produced. As for the case of numerous illegitimate children expected to be looked after by the parish, that has now gone by the by with the new Bastardy Clause Act of 1834, which made the mother the sole responsibility of these bastards until the child is 16 years old - the sole reason being to discourage illegitimate offspring. Birth of an illegitimate child would be deemed to be the mother's own lack of Christian morals and ungodly behaviour for getting herself into such difficulties and would discourage women from entering into profligate relationships. I presume this has gone a long way to bringing down illegitimacy in parishes as a mother of an illegitimate child would get no help."

Mr Adderley interjected, "From what I understand, the workhouse was meant to prove beneficial to the industrious poor, to - operate as a check on those who only used relief because they were too idle to work, and, at the same time be the means of greatly reducing the rates. In the '32-5 period five rates had to be levied to meet the costs of poor relief - £8,000 on out-relief and £1,200 on workhouse relief, don't you know."

Listening in to this, I felt so relieved I had paid employment in this day and age and didn't have to resort to the workhouse. I had no friends or family to rely on and,

God forbid, I'd been attacked and raped and found myself pregnant or found myself in such dire straits that I would have had to accept payment for sex, just to feed myself. If I were pregnant, without a husband, I would have lost my job immediately and, as there was no longer any parish benefit, I would be quickly on my uppers, not able to find work, starving, homeless and having to apply for assistance at a workhouse, where I'd probably remain until I died, because I'd never be able to get out to find work, not with a young baby, that is. There was no relief for a girl, who had been raped – it was seen to be her fault, her responsibility for getting pregnant. The father had no responsibility whatsoever – he could get as many girls pregnant as he cared to as just go about his business with no worry. What a law! I recalled reading 'Tess of the D'Urbervilles' or poor Fanny in 'Far from the Madding Crowd', having to struggle, heavily pregnant, to reach the workhouse, where, in spite of getting there, both she and the baby died.

Anyway, Mr Adderley was speaking, "Yes, indeed, Mr Heathcote," replied Mr Adderley. "However, the situation with out-relief, before '34, illegitimacy aside, was, if a legitimate father were laid off, there would still be money coming in from the children, no matter how mediocre a sum, and this would be supplemented by out-relief, to keep the wolf from the door, don't you know. With this system of workhouses, the whole family is entered into the workhouse. Therefore, you can reason out that no money is coming in whatsoever and there is no way back. Also, if the children are working in other premises, those other manufacturers lose their child workforce, don't you know."

A print of Chell Workhouse, circa 1839.
www.thepotteries.org

Mr Adderley continued - looking over his little round glasses. "I have also heard that they are a bad lot managing them. Rev Aitkin is on the Board of Guardians at Stoke Workhouse, along with Rev Vale and I have heard talk of dreadful punishments taking place. So dreadful that people have actually nicknamed it 'The Bastille'. They feel the place so much resembles a prison and the inmates are treated as prisoners. On entry, they are put into a cellar, stripped and washed and dressed in workhouse clothes and then separated, don't you know. Here, with inmates all dressed the same, it seems that their identity is taken away from them, verily as in a prison. There are numerous rules and regulations, which are disobeyed at the worker's peril. The food is also not more than an unappetising broth or gruel, so foul that you would literally have to be starving, in order to eat it. The very thought of it churns my stomach, and the inmates are submitted to hard labour or put to picking oakum out of old ropes, if they are too infirm for breaking up stone."

"Yes," Mr Peake added, "I have heard of a boy, who tried to escape – and I believe this is just one of many examples. The boy was caught and brought back, where he was stripped to the waist. It seems then that a whole ceremony takes place in these instances. A birch-rod, that had been dripped with salt water, was set on a long table. An audience of officers, clergyman and the governor of the Bastille were brought in. The governor made a speech about the crime of running away and, when he had spoken for a fair time, the clergyman, began speaking, expressing the same sentiments; and then the boy was brought in, scared witless, and laid face down on the table. Four boys were commanded to step forward and hold tightly the arms and legs of the lad. His breeches were next pulled down his legs. Then the rod was raised and it descended, swishing, until blood began to flow. The blows only ceased when the screams of the young lad grew feebler, then ceased."

There were murmurs of disagreement and disbelief following this story of Mr Peake's.

Mr Rose, who had been listening in, joined the group. He stated, in a rather booming voice, standing erect. "It is not just the punishment meted out at these establishments. They were meant to be places for those who were on their uppers and could not afford to pay their rents. Inside they were to do jobs, mainly menial, with some hard labour, for which the tenants were able to earn a pittance that they could build up in order to return to the outside world."

"Now, now, Mr Rose," interrupted Mr Peake, "we're not in court here. Please lower your voice, otherwise I fear the party will be halted."

"I apologise, just my natural way, what hum. However, I'll continue and try to restrain my enthusiasm." In fact Mr Rose turned to look for seating and beckoned the others to take seats too. "I find it difficult to discuss matters while standing, without speaking loudly – part of my military training, what hum." Mr Rose continued in as sotto voce as he could muster. "It has come to my attention that this is not happening. In fact, any pittance earned is put to pay for the incumbent's stay and food while there, so there is no money left over and, in fact, the upkeep of the workhouse is more than these inmates can earn. For a start, my good men, I am not aware if you are cognisant that many arriving at these workhouses are half starved already and ill, or have some mental deficiency that prevents them from working. Other workmates are put to tending these people and are therefore, themselves, not earning money for the workhouse, or indeed put to cooking or cleaning and, again, not earning money. There is little likelihood, therefore, that they can ever return to the outside world and fend for themselves."

"Yes," replied Mr Peake, "I have also heard of weavers whose jobs are now being taken over by mechanical devices. They are applying for assistance; plus I have heard of an elderly lady, so is being forced out of work as her eyesight has deteriorated to such a degree that she can no longer see to work. She applied to a workhouse and was told to go away as she was deemed fit to work. The workhouse was her last resort – no-one applies there now unless they are at their wits end as to how to survive. There was nothing for this elderly lady to do but find a place to curl up and expire. Surely, we should not be hearing such stories, such repercussions, concerning a system the government has put in place, which was meant to help such needy cases?"

Everyone there agreed. For myself, I wasn't totally shocked. Yes, I'd heard about the workhouses and seen various films, notably Dicken's 'Oliver', with little Oliver asking for more gruel, and plenty of other newsreels. There were also still plenty of old buildings around still bearing the words, 'Work is Freedom' above the portals, having once been workhouses, and stories about people tracing their family trees, only to find that one section of the family had been assigned to a workhouse. I believe I remember Barbara Windsor discovering her family, part of the painter, Constable's family, having succumbed to having enter the workhouse.

Mr Meigh had been listening in to this conversation too. "I believe all this talk has made you solemn and miserable, Jane, and we should whisk you away to Strauss' "Blue Danube", which I believe Mr Clementson is at this moment attempting to play on the piano."

I agreed to waltz, yet again, with Mr Meigh.

I approached Mr Meigh in conversation, while dancing, "At various points this evening I have been listening into conversations, not only on the situation with regard to poor people applying to workhouses for their survival but on the political situation in the area at present, although I believe both to be connected. It seems to me that there could possibly be some tinder ready to be lit, in other words, a lot of unrest that could escalate out of hand into riots and mayhem. I would be grateful for your views on the subject, as I feel quite unnerved at the prospect."

"Certainly, Jane, and your metaphor of the fire tinder is indeed just. There is quite a bit of nervousness in town, with the Chartists ready to light the wick to set the whole town alight."

Just then Mr Meigh grabbed me by the hand and pulled me after him, out of the room, into his office. I was, naturally, taken aback by his roughness and tried to pull away. I did not know what his intensions were. The only time I'd been pulled quickly into another room, away from prying eyes was for some fumbling kissing but I couldn't imagine this of Mr Meigh, I mean he was so very much older, at least 30 years. I looked into his eyes – they were startling blue - the first time I'd really studied him. He seemed excited, still holding onto my hand. I could feel a tremble through his fingers, but I read a hesitance on his face to say or do anything. There was a sort of tenderness, but he held back. Maybe he saw the shocked look in my expression, a stiffening in my body as I, at last, tried to free myself from his grasp.

"Oh, I'm sorry, Jane, did I hurt you?" as he released me. "I don't seem to know my own strength….he hesitated as though trying to think of what to say. Finally he managed to compose himself and said, "I was so taken aback with your interest in local events, I couldn't resist in providing you with further information, that I am sure will interest you." At that, he produced some newspapers from his desk.

"Here's a report about the new workhouse." He was looking through the report, "…..yes, here it is…. 'but it may perhaps answer the design of the legislature, to suppress indiscriminate pauperism, by throwing the utmost difficulty in the way of applicants for relief by dealing it out with niggard hand and by prison-like discipline to which claimants must submit, whose necessities oblige them to avail themselves on the House of Refuge.

We are informed that the cost on this palatial structure, for such it seems, with the site and furniture, will not be less than ten thousand pounds, an amount that must preclude any mitigation of the parish-burdens for many years'.

And here a few other reports that have appeared in newspapers.

The Leeds Mercury headlined that 4,025 families in Leeds, one-fifth of the population, are now dependent on parochial relief.

The Stockport Chronicle stated that the pauperism in that town is increasing! Delegates from the manufacturing districts were received at a meeting of Dissenting ministers in London, yesterday; and a Provisional Committee was appointed to prepare some public movement."

"So," I said to Mr Meigh, "this talk of overcrowded workhouses is not just here. It seems to be over the North of England as well."

"Yes, the Chartists are preaching all over the north and into Scotland and Wales. I believe it is their intension, imminently, to derail the workhouses and call a national strike, creating great financial backlash to the government, in order to get their Charter through parliament."

"Can they do that?"

"I do not personally think they have the means or weaponry to succeed. The government forces will stop any uprisings. Unfortunately, the iron trade here has not been able to compete with the low prices of iron in Wales and Scotland, meaning lay-offs of men in the neighbourhood. There have been a couple of pay decreases in consequence and the people are finding things very hard. Everything has a knock-on effect – what affects the iron works, also affects coal and pottery works. Added to that, the grain crops have failed on and off since the disastrous harvest of '37. But the world of business goes in swings and roundabouts and slack periods are to be expected. We're all, well most of us (Mr Meigh peeked around the door, possibly to Mr Broade), are awaiting Robert Peel to review changes to foreign policy. He wishes to introduce free trade and repeal the Corn Laws, but he's up against some strong opposition from his own party. Free trade would give our industry a kick-start and get things moving again, and soon, otherwise I can foresee disastrous consequences."

At that moment we heard voices coming through and sounds of people saying farewell. "It looks as though my guests are leaving. I must go and give my respects to them for attending. Jane, can you please assist with their coats and accessories?" With that, he gently kissed my hand and departed.

So, that was the end of an eventful and interesting evening. I finally left with Mrs Meigh to help her to her room, with John's assistance.

CHAPTER 6

I t wasn't until the Tuesday that I next saw Mr Meigh. We acknowledged each other when passing in a corridor but then Mr Meigh stopped and called me back. "Jane, I have neglected to thank you for your assistance at the soirée on Saturday."

"I thank you sir, but we have not met again until just this moment. This has been your first opportunity."

"Quite so but I would also like to say that you impressed me greatly and, of course, your assistance with my wife."

"Thank you, sir."

"You held yourself with aplomb, although I trust you were entertained. I certainly enjoyed our dances together."

"Most certainly, sir. I thank you again." I didn't know where this was leading so continued, "I believe your wife is waiting for me to commence her exercises, if you could excuse me, sir."

"By all means, Jane. I apologise, I did not wish to apprehend you from your duties. However, I would just like to add that I noticed you were listening intently to the machinations of parliament, as expressed by Mr Sparrow Wilkinson and also views expressed on the likelihood, or not, of uprisings by the unfortunate masses in the neighbouring areas, spurred on by the preachings of the Chartists."

"Yes, sir, I was extremely interested." I, naturally, couldn't tell him that I was trying to find a way back to my own time, by any means possible, and that knowledge of future events to come, might hold the key.

Well, Jane, there have been disturbances in the area, which started yesterday and are continuing. An extraordinary Magistrates' meeting has been called for tomorrow morning at Caverswall. I cannot offer you a seat at the table but, if you wish, you could come along as a servant to assist with beverages and the like. I'm sure another pair of hands would be welcomed. You would then get a chance to listen into proceedings. Naturally, I will have to swear you to not broach a word of the proceedings elsewhere. Every word said at that meeting would be classed as secret. Now Jane, it is all I can offer you at present, but, if you are interested, you may attend. What do you say?"

"I would be most honoured, sir."

"Well done, Jane. I would not expect less of you. I will collect you tomorrow."

Mr Meigh drove me in his carriage to Caverswall. He had presented me with a dark grey, ankle-length, cotton dress, which unlike servants' wear at the time, had strands of silk running through it and a frilled border eight inches up from the ankle. This was an expensive dress for a servant. I was also presented with a white, bibbed apron and a dark grey cotton cap to complement the dress, both having frilled borders.

Extraordinary Magistrates' Meeting,
Wednesday morning, 13th July at Caverswall

Present at the meeting were Job Meigh Esq, T B Rose Esq, R Adderley Esq, Capt Powys, Sir Smith-Child, J A Wise Esq, P B Broade Esq, R E Heathcote Esq, Mr Rhodes (Hanley police), Charles Meigh Esq., Bailiff and Mayor (Mr Job Meigh's brother).

Mr Job Meigh was presiding as Chair. Charles Meigh took the minutes.

Obviously I recognised Mr Rose, from Mr Meigh's soiree and, as my glance went round the table I recognised Mr Heathcote oh and Mr Adderley and Sir Smith-Child. Mr Rose smiled at me, which was nice.

Job Meigh read out, "This meeting has been called due to the disturbed state of the district and further protection being requested by several gentlemen, who consider their property in danger. We firstly request a report on the atrocities at the various collieries in the area and ask Mr Rhodes, of the Hanley Police Constabulary to present his report.

Mr Rhodes commenced, "I have compiled the following account from police operating in Hanley and surrounding districts and reports from colliery owners and their agents:

On Monday, 11th July, a committee of Operative Colliers went to Mr C J Smith's colliery at Longton. Mr Burgess, Mr Smith's agent, asked what they wanted. The reply of one of the leaders was that they wanted an eight-hour day and to be paid 4s a day, free coal, to be paid in cash, and that five nights' work should be paid as six days. Mr Burgess said he couldn't allow anything of the kind and the men decided to break open the engine house door, sent some of their own party into the pits and compelled every man to come up and leave his work. In the scuffle that took place, Mr Burgess was thrown down and kicked and otherwise much abused. They then went onto Mr Sparrow's works. His men were forced out of the pits. Some started to agree with Mr Smith's terms but two or three of these men were ducked in the engine pool. Having completely stopped the work, they proceeded to Mossfield colliery, the Dividy Lane, the Bentilee, Ubberley and Ridgeway collieries at Bucknall. At the last two, men were not at work, but at the others the men were compelled to leave the pits and threatened with mischief if they resumed labour until they gave them leave.

On Tuesday, 12th July, the same lawless course was pursued by these misguided men. The Longton colliers went to Wiaton's Wood where they were met by men from other places. They forcibly drove men out from Fenton Park works, and compelled some of them to go along with them. In visiting Lord Granville's works, they were disappointed in finding all at rest and none of the colliers at work. At a pit near Mr Hackwood's works, they broke into the engine house, got the steam up, started the engine and did much wilful mischief to the machinery. At the Bells Mill pit they burst open the engine-house door and broke up the floor in search of the engine-man. At the Beoden Brook Pit, I and two of my Hanley police colleagues, Mr Hilton and Mr Geoestry were on the spot, with a view to watch their proceedings. On seeing them we swore not to have any constables there to drive them off. Resistance to such numbers would have been fruitless and we were obliged to leave them to do as they liked. We were severely pelted with stones as we retired from the ground. During the day, the colliers at Bucknall, Norton, Cobridge and Tunstall were visited by the same or other mobs and the men forced to desist from work and leave the pits."

"Thank you, Mr Rhodes. As you can see, gentlemen, from Mr Rhodes detailed report, some immediate action is required. In my opinion these unlawful mobs will not desist and will not obey the police with orders to disband. I, therefore, see no other option than to call for the aid of the military. I trust all of you agree to this action." All present nodded their agreement. Mr Meigh continued, "The Newcastle and Pottery troup of Yeomanry, have been given notice to be in readiness and I will forthwith summon them into action and to remain under arms during the night. I also believe a detachment of 12th foot under the command of Captain Granet, consisting, I've been told, about 120 men can be called on to assist. They are based at Weedon Barracks. If a special train is laid on they could get to us by 3am tomorrow. All in favour of marshalling these troops say 'Aye'." A shout of 'Aye' went up and this was recorded. Mr Meigh went on to say that a printed proclamation should be issued, declaring their determination to make use of the force at their disposal for the punishment of offenders and for the protection of the well-disposed, who might peaceably return to their employment. This was noted and agreed for Charles Meigh to attend to.

Capt. Powys spoke, "I have on stand-by infantry and troop of Yeomanry commanded by Lieutenant Wilkinson. I suggest we should meet at 3 o'clock today in Stoke and proceed to Longton at their head."

All agreed and the meeting was brought to a close.

There was another extraordinary meeting planned for the Friday. I was to attend again. This meeting was to be in Newcastle.

Magistrates' meeting at Newcastle
Friday 15ᵗʰ July

Present at the meeting were Job Meigh Esq, T B Rose Esq, R Adderley Esq, Capt Powys, Sir Smith-Child, J A Wise Esq, P B Broade Esq, R E Heathcote Esq, Mr Rhodes (Hanley police), Charles Meigh Esq, Bailiff and Mayor.

The minutes of Wednesday's meeting were read.

Charles Meigh excused himself from taking the minutes. He had borne some injuries at Longton, having been stoned by the mob and his right arm was in a sling.

Capt Powys asked the committee for someone else to take the minutes. There was a short discussion as to who would take this on. Suddenly, I heard myself saying, "I'll take the minutes, sirs..." and then more quietly, "If I may, if this is not unseemly." A room of astonished faces regarded me, mouths agape.

Job Meigh came to my rescue. "That is very honourable of you, Jane. I know you are well-read and interested in these proceedings. It would certainly assist us greatly to enable us all to concentrate on the proceedings." To the room, "Does anyone here have any objections to my er …. Jane, taking the minutes?

There was another mumble of voices, 'unheard of, unprecedented, what, what, a woman!' but it was finally agreed, as Job Meigh seemed to have confidence in my abilities, for me to take the minutes and I removed my apron and picked up pencil a paper.

Capt. Powys presided as Chair.

"As you know, we proceeded with the infantry and Yeomanry from Stoke to Longton on Wednesday. Unfortunately, we did not meet up with any lawless mobs. It seems that a great many of the colliers went to Cheadle and those who remained manifested no disposition to try their strength with the military. There was some disturbance, however, as we returned in the evening to Newcastle, being pelted with stones at Longton, however, no mischief was done.

Job Meigh at this point got to his feet, in the pretence of stretching his legs. He looked over at my scribblings and I could feel, if not see, a shocked look come across his face.

"What do you call these preposterous scribblings, miss? Are you the work of the devil? Have you devised this plot to defame me? Then, out of the blue I found myself scudding across the floor. I'd been heftily smacked across the head and knocked off my chair. I yelped. I was in pain. Job Meigh was shouting for me to get out of his sight and never show my evil face again and continued to aim further slaps and punches.

I was holding my head, trying to bring myself to some form of consciousness as to what had happened, and curled up to try to defend myself.

I managed to blurt out, stuttering "I'm using …Pitman's short…hand…. sir. I have no … intention of ….defaming you. I can read back everything…. that has been said so far, sir."

At that point, Mr Rose spoke up, "Mr Meigh. Please desist in this assault, what hum. I believe the girl is right."

"Eh, how can she possibly be right, sir. She has written a load of scribbles."

"As it appears to you, Mr Meigh. But I believe the girl is right by mentioning this Mr Pitman as this name has brought to mind that I recall hearing the name and that he has created a new form of short writing, a 'shorthand' as it has come to be known. He has set up quite a few schools in London lately and, as the young miss has come from London, she may have been enrolled into one of his schools. I think we should hear from her directly."

Mr Meigh was still too outraged to speak so Mr Rose stood and got me to my feet. "Is this true that you have undertaken a course of this 'shorthand' in one of Mr Pitman's schools?"

"…. Yes, sir." I replied shakily. I apologise for having caused such a disturbance but, if you will bear with me, I will read back the comment Capt Powys made.

"That would be fitting," Mr Rose replied.

I hastily got my book and pencil together, while Mr Rose righted my chair, and began to read back my shorthand.

'As you know, we proceeded with the infantry and Yeomanry from Stoke to Longton on Wednesday. Unfortunately, we did not meet up with any lawless mobs. It seems that a great many of the colliers went to Cheadle and those who remained manifested no disposition to try their strength with the military. There was some disturbance, however, as we returned in the evening to Newcastle, being pelted with stones at Longton, however, no mischief was done.'

I stopped and looked around at the committee. All seemed to be nodding in agreement except Mr Job Meigh who held his head down.

Mr Rose continued, "Hrmhh (cough). I can see from your acknowledgements that our young lady has done a good job, in fact word for word as to Capt Powys commencement speech and believe that we should allow Jane to continue taking the minutes, what hum.

All said "Ay", even Job Meigh. I did not get an apology. So, I'd got first hand an example of his cruelty. Mrs Chetwynd had told me to beware not to annoy him as he's 'not afraid to lash out'.

Capt Powys continued:

"About 9pm yesterday, our military force was augmented by the arrival of the Congleton troup of the Cheshire Yeomanry, under the command of Lieutenant W S Reade, making altogether a formidable array of military power. It seems that the colliers assembled early in the morning in great numbers on Crown Bank, Hanley, most of them armed with sticks. A mob went to the Chapel Field, where several men were loading carts with coals. Two of them were dragged off to pits of water in the neighbourhood and forced into them and made dip overhead. A similar outrage was perpetrated on a man at a colliery in Far Green. The populace, who had assembled in great numbers, appeared to approve heartily of this outrageous and cowardly conduct, and the excitement was so great that the Chief Bailiff considered it his duty to require the Magistrates to send the military over, with which request they immediately complied. Most magistrates here seated assembled about 12 noon with the whole force in the High Street and marched directly to Hanley. There we found a great crowd collected and a very hostile feeling prevailing. In consequence of the mob beginning to pelt the soldiers, the Riot Act was read and the former, fearing what might follow, scampered off in all directions. The soldiers returned to Newcastle about 3pm.

Mr Rhodes (Hanley police) was asked next to give an up-to-date report.

"I have further to report that, on Wednesday morning, of 13th July, apart from the outrage and Riot Act being read at Hanley, as Capt. Powys just reported, at an early hour, a large body of miners again assembled at Longton and, having satisfied themselves that there was no work going on at the collieries in that neighbourhood, proceeded to follow up their plan at stopping the works at places which they had not yet visited.

A party went to some of the pits in the neighbourhood of Cheadle. Some carts that were going to the collieries there from the Potteries they turned back and one loaded cart they upset in the road. Mr Kinnersley's pits, at Kidsgrove, were visited in the course of the day. They also went to Mr Heathcoat's at Apedale, and Mr Sneed's at Silverdale and told the men what they might expect if they went to work the next morning. In the evening a large body assembled in Hanley Market Place, but no breech of the peace took place.

On Thursday, 14th July, a number of men went again to the neighbourhood of Cheadle and succeeded in stopping such of the collieries as were still at work. At one of the pits, where they thought the engine-tender had deceived them, they, without ceremony, threw him into the engine pit and put their own men into the engine-house and wound up the men and horses from the pits. In the evening, a Chartist named Ellis, from Burslem, addressed a crowd of persons in the Hanley Market Place; and Cambell, another Chartist, lectured at the George and Dragon, in that town. Numbers of colliers were walking about in the various towns, many of them begging and most of them carried thick sticks or bludgeons. In Cheadle a party heard that the bailiffs were in procession of property near the church year. They went there and demanded the bailiffs leave the property. They then commenced a most outrageous and brutal attack on their person, beating them with their sticks and bludgeons most desperately. Two of them were severely wounded and barely escaped with their lives. All the collieries are closed in the neighbourhood."

Capt Powys continued. "I would like to add, that it has become known to me that Her Majesty, Queen Victoria is aware of the Chartist activities and the attacks that have been carried out. She has written to Sir Robert Peel, that she was surprised at the little or no opposition to the disgraceful activities and the passiveness of the troops. She said there should be action by the troops to prevent meetings. Everything should be done to apprehend Cooper and all his delegates, who were members of the Chartist movement. The Home Secretary had written to magistrates throughout the country, telling them to suppress all large meetings, regardless of their character and let the troops act with vigour and without parley. That being said, we will, obviously, do our utmost to obey her Majesty's rulings, but unfortunately the military have become cautious of moving around at night following the incident in Stone a couple of years ago. If you recall, in this incident cavalry had been attacked in the streets from behind barricades. Traps had been set to pull horses to the ground and a number of soldiers had been badly injured. This type of attack has now become known as 'guerrilla warfare' so named from a pamphlet we came across by the Italian revolutionary Francis Maceroni called 'Defensive Instruction For The People', a sort of layman's guide to urban guerrilla warfare. Another pamphlet had come into our possession at the time, published by the radical Alexander Somerville – a counter pamphlet 'Warnings To The People On Street Warfare' These are not necessarily linked to the Chartist speeches, there is no proof, but we certainly should be wary of such guerrilla warfare strategies and keep careful watch over Chartist activity."

Capt Powys closed the meeting, stating that military forces would remain on full alert until further notice. He also added that there were a number of people who had been arrested, including Edward Sale, who was caught at the race course camp. It was believed that he had been sent, by the Chartist movement, to spy on the military. The magistrates would be sentencing these people in court.

I wasn't sure, after the meeting ended, whether or not I was still working for Mr Meigh and if I would get a lift back. Mr Meigh had said nothing. My face was still stinging and I was aching. I followed Mr Meigh and, gratefully, he assisted me into the carriage. After some minutes on the journey, Mr Meigh spoke.

"I do not have to apologise for my actions, Jane. You are a servant and can expect my disapproval if I am seen to be taken advantage of or made to look unwise in my actions."

I went to speak but he stopped me. "Please do not interrupt….. Your scribblings, Pitman's shorthand, whatever you call it, appeared to me on first sight as an absolute an act of sabotage and I was enraged beyond all comprehension. As you proved yourself at the meeting, not to be committing a gross outrageous act, as first thought, I forgive you and wish you to continue in your current position at Ash Hall. Unfortunately, I am not an easy man when provoked and quick to anger, which can develop into physical tirades. I trust I have not hurt you beyond repair and that your bruises will heal in good time…… Jane, I apologise. There I've said it……I like you Jane, and respect you and, if there is any way I can make it up to you, I will try."

At that point Mr Meigh, pulled me towards him and kissed me firmly on the lips. I pushed him back as forcibly as I could and wiped the back of my hand over my lips.

"Mr Meigh, stop, please stop. You are out of order….. First you attack me and now you want to make amorous advances towards me. What sort of man are you? You think you can have everything your own way. Well, you're not going to. You're married, Mr Meigh, sir, kindly remember that. I cannot be taken advantage of in that way. I will leave your service forthwith. Just drive me to the Hall and I will collect my belongings"

"Oh, Jane, I find myself apologising yet again, but you cannot have missed that I am entranced by you. You have bewitched me and I find I can no longer control myself. You say I am married, but that marriage no longer holds anything for me. My wife will not even look at me. That is no comfort for a man. I need the tenderness of a woman, someone I can hold passionately and relay my thoughts and feelings to; and I find myself drawn to you, to your sympathy and understanding, your kindness, even to your enquiring nature and understated handsomeness. There is something in your smile, alluring. Please kiss me, Jane."

"Let me go, Mr Meigh. You are mistaken in your concepts that my kindness and sympathy have been directed in anyway as amorous feelings for you. I insist you must control yourself. I am not of the same mind. I have no feelings for you. I am only here for a short time, hopefully, and will leave as soon as I possibly can."

CHAPTER 7

"**T**ha knows that wuz no 'accident' sithee, with Mrs Meigh oither." John whispered to me when I was back at Ash Hall. "Ah wos thar. Don't let on tha knows or ''ay'll ev thay guts fer garters."

"What do you mean, John, no 'accident?"

"They woz 'eving sich a blooming row the pair of 'em. Don't know what it woz abite, wasn't that close up to 'ere – just 'eard the bawling. Master gets out of the cart, then meks a grab for the Mistress, pulled 'er rite bodily off the cart. Smack on the grind shay went, yed ferst en the grind was frozzen 'erd, baying February. Shay ley thar som taim, not mooeving. 'ay jest walks eff. Ah grabs 'er oop and teks har insaid to har room. Dinah tended har, but shay's nivver bayn the seme sence.

Just as I turned to go indoors my glance led me over the fields and down to the Hanley, and Burslem parts of Stoke-on-Trent. I looked aghast. "John, look there's a huge fire in the town. It looks like the whole of Stoke is on fire, the whole town is blanketed in smoke. We must do something"

"War hast thay bayn ducky? Thut tha is the Potteries. Theer's hundreds of little potbanks en bottle ovens belch'ng ite smok, chokking the very brith ite o' ever a one theer.

'owivver, it mayt be chockking the loif ite 'f the workers but it's 'ow fokks mek a living, put fooed on'table. The Master 'ad his warks dine theer too. Et's not a pleece fer thay te bay, ducky. Et's darty and rakes 'f homanity, if tha noss whats ah mane, conna say nay mer to a lady, wodna be raight.

Also, theer's bayn som going's on dine thar o' leet wi' the cowl moiners. Arly lest month 300 cowl moiners went on stroik far Mr Spooner's pits. ay cµt thar wages fer 3s 7d a dee te jest 3s. Thee conna live on that. Thee conna afford bread te eat en peey thar rent. A wake or mer leeter the moiners war stopping min fer warking at the manes. En Lard Shelton's warks at Shelton cµt wages bay 6d a dee. Moiners and iron warkers stopped th'engines, pulled plµgs fer the boilers. Thµt maent thar wuzna cowl, sow th'pits en potbanks conna bay fayered, sow thes led te 5000 warkers oot on stroik. Thar's bin thoosands ef warkers applying fer assistance at th'wark'ises avery dee.

Ah tells thay what, ah've family in Tunster. Ah'll tek thay tha en thay con tok te'em – git an idea loik as te what's goin' on."

"Sure, that sounds like a good idea. Maybe we can go on the 25th July, Sunday, our day off."

Maybe I had to go to the Potteries, I thought to myself. Maybe I'd find the reason there why I'd been brought back to the 19th century. Was there something else I had to do? John had made a means for Mrs Meigh to get downstairs and her exercises were helping, and I hadn't returned to my time, so that wasn't it. What was happening back in my own time? Had they missed me? Were they looking for me? Would I still have a job to go back to? I had to find out the reason I was here, and that thick, toxic fog down the hill might have the answer. I was desperate to get back to my own time.

So, Sunday 25th July came and John and I set out down Ash Bank Road for Tunstall (I realised John's Tunster must be his pronunciation of Tunstall). We were heading for Hanley, then would turn north to Tunstall.

Ash Bank was not as I recognised it, with its little Victorian terraces. Ash Bank was just a road leading from Hanley to Cheadle and Ashbourne in the East. The Victorian terraces were no longer there. There were just fields, farms and woodland on either side of the road instead. I realised that the terraces must have been built after this time and I recalled now seeing some date plaques on the buildings, stating they had been built in 1879. As we neared Hanley I could feel the smoke tingling in the back of my throat. It felt like it was clinging to my clothes. We were walking through a dense mist and I couldn't see far, probably 50 yards, before everything went into a blur of indistinguishable grey. There were a few trees and plants trying to survive, but they were blighted – black spots on the few leaves they produced and the grass, a blackened, sickly yellow colour. All the houses on the way were covered in a film of black coal, there was no colour, just shades of black and grey. The people we passed along the way looked shrivelled up, bent over, hopeless, ashen figures. The tramps I'd seen in London, begging on the streets, looked healthier.

We finally arrived at Tunstall and I was introduced to John's family, his brother, Jimmy, Jimmy's wife Joan and some of their children – Charlie (about 10), Willie (about 12), Lizzie (about 8), Ann (about 6) and Mary (about 4). They all looked half-starved and their clothes were in tatters.

The house was a very rough hovel, two up and two down. There was nothing in the way of home comfort that I could see. No carpet or lino – just rough quarry tiles. There was a sturdy table with chairs in the main room downstairs, and a huge hearth with cast iron fireplace and range, which burnt coal, and was used for cooking. There was a rough wooden table in the back room, a pantry and a sink, but no taps for running water. Upstairs I presumed there were two rooms for sleeping for the whole family. There may have been a coal fire up there too, but I didn't get to see. The walls had wood panelling on the lower half with bare plaster on the top half. There was a picture rail around the main room but wasn't being used. Everything again was covered in a fine film of coal dust, mainly, I presumed, because of the fire. I'm sure Joan did her best to try to keep it clean but I could see that it would be a thankless task.

"Ow at thee ducks? Com sit thee sen dine." Joan indicated to a chair. "Dost tha want a dish o' tea? Ah conna affer yer onything else mind."

"Yes, thank you, that would be nice after the long walk".

"Thay'll not bay fer 'ereaboots, ah can 'ear".

"No, from London".

"Yer, thet'll be eet. What's tha doin' 'ere?"

I went on to explain where I was working and that's where I'd met John. I added that I wanted to get an idea of what was happening in the collieries and potbanks.

"Well, fayther's in the cowl" she pointed to Jimmy. "ay's oota werk. Aw th moiners er on straik fer mer brass. Tha've cμt tha peey en want 'em te werk longer μrhs. Way codna live on what ay browt whom afore sow thar've aw com μt. Dμnna neow 'ow eet'll werk μt. Way 'atna a pot te piss in now en ah'm afeared things'll jest get woss owe rate. War clean bart monny and clemmed.

Th childer con tawk te yer abµt tha werk in't potbank. Charlie, Willie, Ann and Lizzie werks tha. Mary's at skol. But th elders 'o 'em are µt 'o werk too, az th moiners spoiled the potbanks en thah's nay cowl te fire 'em enywise. Ef way donna get nay brass soon, ah con see owl o'us goin' te Chell werk'ise. Jimmy en me er at ow wits end." I could see she was getting very distressed and rose to try to comfort her.

"Tok te Charlie, ay con tok yer leg af ef yer let 'em."

My attention went to the children. They didn't look their ages, small, stunted, very thin. They were bare-footed and their clothes were in tatters and dirty.

I started talking to Charlie while the others played marbles – or chuck I' th' 'ole, as they called it. They were made of plain alabaster – not the marbles I remembered in my youth, which were made of glass with what resembled the iris of a cat's eye in the centre of the marble, of varying colours. Every so often one would call out, but with no seeming energy to their voices, "Crogs, no peys", which I gleaned meant the marble had moved but there would be no forfeit, and "knockle darn, nay funking", which I've no idea about, and "rinkers", which I gathered were the larger marbles.

Charlie had a very sad story to tell. He'd gone to Old Betty W's school, where Mary attended now. Betty was a benevolent old lady giving lessons in the only room on the ground floor of her little cottage. His education was considered complete after three or four years and he was then deemed ready to start work. A neighbour suggested he start work as a mould runner. Her son was an apprentice muffin-maker at the same potbank – it was his job to craft plates of less than seven inches in diameter. He'd been there a few months now – started when he turned 10. I asked him how long he was expected to work each day and got the appalling answer that he had to be there at 5 in the morning to light the fire in the stove room so it was hot enough for the master to start work at 6am, and he couldn't leave before 8pm, more probably didn't get home again until 9 or 10pm. For that he got the princely sum of one shilling a week.

A mould runner, which was the job Charlie had been employed to do, had to carry the clay plates the muffin-maker made, to a bottle oven or stove room. The stove room was a small room with shelves all around where the plaster moulds were placed to allow the soft clay to dry.

In the centre of the room was a piping hot iron stove "full of fire", with an iron pipe, which led to the chimney. Describing his work, Charlie said it was not an unusual thing for this stove and the chimney pipe to be red with the intense heat of the fire.

It was his job to place the plaster moulds on the shelves, on their edge, slightly leaning against the wall, so as to get the full surface heat and to avoid damage to the soft place on the moulds. A small pair of wooden steps was available so he could reach the higher shelves in this stove room. He had to run up these steps for all the higher shelves, say one-fifth of the whole number. He had then to run to his 'master' with an empty mould, and return with a full one to the stove room. The job was properly called mould-running, as he had to run there, run back, run there, run back continuously. He would be kept going for twenty minutes or half-an-hour at a time, the sweat coursing down his face and back, making rivulets of perspiration on both.

When enough plates had been made and dried, he carried them back to his master to be 'backed' on a whirligig, when the plate could be smoothed.

Charlie would then carry them back one by one to the stove room for further drying. The moulds could then be taken out and gathered into 'bungs' of about two dozen plates, ready for 'fettling', that is, trimming or cleaning the rough edges of the plate, reading for firing.

"Ah'd hef to run in en out o' the stove room, winter en summer wi' ets blazing 'ot stove. Ef ah wizna fast enough, me master wud gee me whut fer, 'cos et 'eld 'im up in 'is wark en ay'd git whut fer frµm the boss all aleng o' may, en a feew tarms ah've bin 'it en cossed ef ah wizzna back in tarm. Ah was bad once en codna keep up, hed a cold or sommink en ah got sech a swipe et knocked me sure af me feet. But ah was drippin' in sweat en feeling cold et the seeme tarm. Ah werrit awt tarm that ay's gonna kicky shed may or gee may a leathering."

This fettling was the last process of the day's work, and a comparatively easy time for both master and Charlie, and very welcome as both were exhausted by the long, hard labour of the day.

'Wedging' clay was one of the toughest jobs. "Me ouder bruvver, Harry, des thet job, e's 14. Et teks a lot 'o strength en 'im baying 'alf-fed', loik may, ay jest donna 'ev th'energy" said Charlie. The wedger takes a lump of raw clay upon a plaster block, cuts it in two with a piece of wire, lifts one half above his head, and then brings it down upon the lower half, to mix them, with whatever force he can command.

This had to be repeated until the clay was brought to the consistency of something like putty. Doing such work as this was 'rest' from the mould-running.

His mother interrupted at this point. "Yer, oll o' em com back efter a day's wark, senatucked. Ow Charlie teks a snappin te wark but somtarms dosna git tarm t'eat it. Ah meek em thar stir-pudding but thar nah asleep afore finishing et. Et's no reet. Ah 'as te carry 'em te bed. Et fair meeks may weep but way canna do nowt. Faither's jest no peeyed enough en neow thay cuts 'is peey. Ah don't know 'ow way're te manage."

James then cut in, "Way'll nivver survive t'wark'ouse. Thah jest fayes 'em on graysey watter en a few lumps o' sommink, thet'd mek a tiger's tayth ache to break t'fibres of! Ah 'ev 'erd payple says eet's brutal. They feed yer nowt te liv bay, jest 'nuf te kayp yer aloive. Fer whut ah've 'erd, jest a hunk o' bread en a jug o' skilly for soopper."

I interrupted, "Sorry, what's skilly, James. I've not come across this term?"

"Weel, ducky, yer nivver want te. Peeg's swill wud test better. Eet's supposed te bay mayle en watter but eet's as though eet's bin left te rot affore boiling – the vilest test yer cud ivver imagine."

He continued, "Thah's a scholl theer - boys git wacked ov'r yed, ov'r en ov'r effin thah a mite slow loik. Na thut oor kids 'r slow. Thee con al rade."

I was really taken aback by this story and almost in tears myself. There was no union in these days, no child protection laws. Machines have now done away with these cruel forms of child-labour, but not in 1842 and not for some while. So, while the great lords and gentlemen who owned the mills and the factories and the coal mines luxuriated in their wealth, giving themselves airs and graces with external appearance of having kind and benevolent hearts, passing laws to prevent the importation of African slaves to America to work in the cotton fields and elsewhere, none of them gave a thought to the 'slaves' they had working under their very noses.

As I later found out, these lords and gentlemen did initiate changes to the mines and cotton mills in Lancashire and Yorkshire some time later. This was mainly because children, as young as 6 years old, were being used, in the cotton mills, to clean up the shreds of material caught under and in the machines, being deemed small enough to get under the machines. This led to many children often getting their hair or fingers caught in the looms and being badly mutilated or even killed. Because of this, the mill owners would tend to use children with no families/orphans for these jobs so, as no-one would miss them. However, these deaths and mutilations eventually came to light and so the mill owners had to be seen to be doing something about this. But for those children in the Potteries, either in the pot-works or brickyards, they were not to see any benefit for many years later. (Note 1)

The father, Jimmy, had been listening in and added his feelings about the situation in the collieries.

"Eet's na jest the moyners 'ere thet're an stroik. Weer colling far a general stroik, al o'er the country en Scotland, en Wales. We'll na go bek 'til thah gee us mer peey. The Charteests 've another bill thar gonna put afore Parliment. Thar've bin preaching al rµnd. 'ere, Ev a read of this." Jimmy started shuffling through papers in a drawer and produced a document, which he handed to me. "This uns fer '38. Eet'll tell yer al abowt whµt we're faiting fer."

I started to read the document, written in 1838 mainly by William Lovett of the London Working Men's Association. It outlined the People's Charter, and detailed the six key pointed that the Chartists believed were necessary to reform the electoral system and thus alleviate the suffering of the working classes – these were:

Universal Suffrage (the right to vote)

Reading through, I discovered that, at the time, only 18% of the adult-male population of Britain could vote – before 1832 this was just 10%. The Charter proposed that the vote be extended to all adult males over the age of 21, apart from those convicted of a felony or declared insane.

No Property Qualification

Potential members of Parliament needed to own property of a particular value. This prevented the vast majority of the population from standing for election. By removing the requirement of a property qualification, candidates for elections would no long have to be selected from the upper classes.

Annual Parliaments

The Charter stated that a government could retain power as long as there was a majority of support. This made it very difficult to replace a bad or unpopular government.

Equal Representation

The 1932 Reform Act had abolished the worst excess of 'pocket boroughs'. A pocket borough was a parliamentary constituency owned by a single patron, who controlled voting rights and could nominate the two members who were to represent the borough in Parliament. In some of these constituencies as few as six people could elect two members of Parliament. There were still great differences between constituencies, particularly in the industrial north where there were relatively few MPs compared to rural areas.

The Chartists proposed the division of the United Kingdom into 300 electoral districts, each containing an equal number of inhabitants, with no more than one representative from each district to sit in Parliament.

Payment of Members

MPs were not paid for the job they did. As the vast majority of people required income from their jobs to be able to live, this meant that only people with considerable personal wealth could afford to become MPs. The Charter proposed that MPs were paid an annual salary of £500.

Vote by Secret Ballot

Voting at the time was done in public, using a 'show of hands' at the 'hustings' (a temporary, public platform from which candidates for parliament were nominated). Landlords or employers could therefore see how their tenants or employees were voting and could intimidate them and influence their decision. **(Note 2)**

The Charter was launched in Glasgow in May 1838, at a meeting attended by an estimated 150,000 people. Presented as a popular-style Magna Carta. It rapidly gained support across the country and its supporters became known as the Chartists. A petition, populated at Chartist meetings across Britain, was brought to London in May 1839, for Thomas Attwood to present to Parliament. It boasted 1,280,958 signatures, yet Parliament voted not to consider it. **(Note 3)**

"Can I take this with me, Jimmy?"

"Thet's owrate, ducky. Ef yer eenterested loik maybe John con breng yer, te one ef th Charteest maitings, ef yer minded."

"Yes, thank you. Hopefully, I'll be able to attend one of them."

Jimmy then turned his attention to the children, "Wot yer's doin' lossocking abowt. Ger outa 'ere en fetch som cowl – ger o'er mowrs en git digging en say wot mer yews con snaffle o' kedge... so skiddaddle. Tek somink te deeg wi', yer mayt find som tatties or carrats int' ferms, but mind yer no sayn. Kayp yer yeds dine."

"But we're starved da, en ah'm jaggled. Con way 'ev a smite afore way goes?"

"Thar's nay smite te be 'ad, Charlie, unless yer gits eet yersel."

All the children picked themselves up slowly, lacking energy to do much else, and went.

He addressed me again. "Donna ef thar knows but thar's top cowl an th'mowrs o'er th bek of the beeg 'owse war thar's et – jest need te deeg fer eet. Thar's nay cowl comin' outa moins sah thet's th best way con do."

"I understand, Jimmy. We must be going now..... John."

I looked towards John to see if that was OK. He nodded. Before we go, I must use your toilet.

".... Oh, thar means th jetty. Eet's owt bek."

I went out the back door and there was a roughly bricked, stand-alone sort of hovel with a rough wooden door. The toilet stank and I could see piles of shit outside in a sort of ditch Looking inside, the 'toilet' was basically a bricked up structure with a hole in the top on which sat a wooden seat surround on which you sat. The 'produce' went into a hole dug in the ground from which ran a narrow ditch lined with a pottery open piping. Water running from a pottery pipe from the kitchen sink was intended to get the 'produce' moving along the ditch, which (I found out later) ran into a sockpit, a pit into which the nightsoil runs. However, I could see that more often or not there wasn't enough water poured down and the produce collected in offensive smelling piles. A nightsoil man would come round regularly to collect the 'soil', which would then be taken to spread as manure over the fields. Of course, this manure wasn't of much use to the crops, but it was a way of getting rid of it.

Hanging from a peg was newspaper, each page of which had been cut into about four pieces. This was presumably for wiping yourself. This went into another bucket. The smell was rife - putrid. I wouldn't have bothered to go but I was desperate.

I couldn't help thinking that the Romans had a sewer system and baths back in the day and yet we hadn't developed a sewerage system nearly two thousand years later. I could see a tin bath hanging up on a hook at the back of the house. They'd probably have to try to heat pans of ditch water over the fire for a bath.

Getting back in the house I heard a man hollering outside in the street.

"Jimmy, move thasen, fetch a bucket. Et's the higgler" Joan shouted. They both got buckets and rushed out of the house. It was apparent that the water man was doing his rounds, selling fresh water. All the neighbours were out there trying to be the first to buy this precious commodity, at ½d a bucket, before it was all gone. This water came all the way from the Washerwall well in Werrington, close to Mr Meigh's house where John and I worked.

On the way home, John and I discussed the miners strike and the influence of the Chartists.

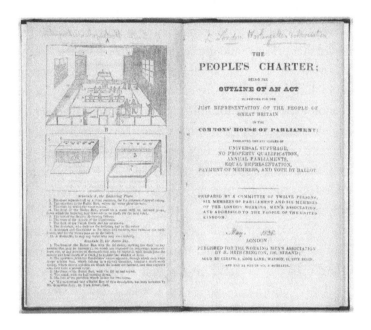

British Library, Shelfmark: 8138 bb87

Discussing the situation with John on the way home, I discovered that 300 colliers at Mr Sparrow's pits in Longton had been on strike for several weeks since the beginning of July 1842. Mr Sparrow had cut their wages from 3s 7d a day to just 3s. He had a legal requirement to give two weeks' notice of this reduction, but chose instead simply to attempt to impose it at once. Sparrow could afford the lock out. Coal prices had dropped and wages were, to his mind, too high, and a lock out at least stopped the wage bill. The reason he gave the colliers for the reduction of their pay was that he was finding the competition in the iron trade so severe in consequences of the low prices of iron at the Welsh and Scotch works, he found it impossible to continue as at present and that the men must either submit to a reduction in the price of their labour or he must blow out his furnaces. He added that prices would get better again in due course; in the meantime, it was to be lower wages, or no wages. He was in no rush to settle. The poor colliers were at the mercy of an economy they could not influence, with masters who would exploit them at any opportunity, and they were left feeling the only way to affect change was by their own militancy.

"Eet's led te a mob of colliers and ithers goin' arund t'deesteekt forcibly stapping mon fer warking et t'pits. Eet's bin reported in't paypers... O' cors, th paypers er al fur Mr Sparrow, thah thenk ay's dun no wrang, ays in't clear. Trµbble es, thot maist folk donna wanna stroik, tha canna afford te bay owta wark. Allus payple er skeered."

John continued saying that Lord Granvill's works at Shelton had become embroiled in the trouble and he, too, had ordered his agent to cut wages - by 6d a day. He had seen his opportunity to drive wages down, and seized it. The men came out. A meeting in Hanley decided that the strike should become general. A committee of Operative Colliers put their demands forward that they wanted an eight hour day and to be paid 4s a day, free coal, to be paid in cash, and that five nights' work should be paid as six days. With intimidation and violence, the colliers succeeded in spreading the strike. The bands of men visited virtually every mine and iron works in the district, stopping engines and pulling plugs from boilers, known as the Plug Plot. Of course, the strikes resulted in a lack of coal. The kilns in the potbanks could not be fired. The pottery workers were unable to work as a result and they joined the ranks of unemployed in the area. It was also reported that the mobs were spreading the strike and forcing even agricultural workers to join the strike. By this time there were some five thousand workers on strike, and many more simply could not work for lack of coal. Men and their families were literally beginning to starve to death from wages so low they could not afford to buy bread.

"Mr Meigh en t'uther mageestraytes colled owt t'yeomanry en troops a couple o' days ago. Thah set up an 'anley race course. Thot fair scuppered the stroikers en som o'm retarned te wark. Th colliery owners promised te luk at thah weshes, so the bands 'o man, demandin' monny wi threats of violence, went wom. But t'owners dinna peey 'em ony mind en en consequence, two peets cam owt en ah 'ear thar's bin trouble en Burslem yastardee."

"Yes, I heard about it…. Jimmy mentioned the Chartists. Who are they and how have they become involved in all this, John?"

"Ah weel, ducky, th Charteests got a Peeple's Charter together in '38 – yer've gor the pamphlet Jimmy giv yer. Thet woz presented te Parlament wi al o' oor weshes, but Parlament rejected eet. But tha havna geen up. Anuther presentation woz made just in May thees yayre – thet wuz rejected too. Th mageestrayes 'r certain th Charteests 've enstigated al o' thayse goings an, saying thar've put spays owt ont military. T'Charteests 've been spayking at rallies en maytings, gitting people rowsed µp. Tha wonna uffer man, en som wimman t'opportunity, wi thees Charter, o' gittin' a vote, gittin' a saiy in oo's elected te parlament – az tha coles eet 'th vote en mer te ate' en th chance te stap 'dying te leev'. Tha wonna present anµther Charter te Parlament."

We got back to Ash Hall and I started reading the paper I'd picked up on Friday, plus I found another one discarded in the lounge.

John knocked on my door. He had found a pamphlet from November 1838, referring to the Chartist leader Feargus O'Connor's speech, when he visited Hanley. Reading through it, it seems there were over five thousand people present. He was there with William Ellis, John Richards and Joseph Capper, all of whom were to become local Chartism speakers. O'Connor addressed the rally with the following words, "Ye have about 130 master potters, who annually share about one million's worth of your labour. Now, £250,000 would be more than ample for risk and speculation, and the remaining £750,000 would make you independent of the three Devil Kings of Somerset House".

"Who does he mean by the three Devil Kings of Somerset House?" I asked John.

"Ah, thayse 'r the thray Poor Law Commissioners in London, ducky." He replied.

I continued reading to discover that it was decided then to elect a delegate to the first Chartist convention, due to be held in the February of 1839. John Richards was nominated and chosen to represent the Potteries. Joseph Capper closed the meeting after five hours, calling for torchlight meetings and a Sacred Week.

"What's a Sacred Week?"

"Ah, thuht's thah weey ef saying thah want te organais a straiyk. Thah've go' togither a petition these yeeyr af ten thusand signatures. Ah belayve thah've gat guns en pikes – thar preparing fer a war. Thah allso telling payple te apply fer poor relief. Ah nahs en Burslem μp te fave honderd new applications fer assistance 'r seen overy deey. Thah conna cope. But, ah belave, thets whut th Charteests want."

John had some other leaflets he'd picked up at various meetings. The general gist of these was that the Potteries were in the grip of the worst trade depression of the nineteenth century and the Chartists were offering hope and opportunity. Working men should have the chance to run their own lives. They believed that if they could develop influence, then they would be able to affect foreign policy, which determined export trade, the life blood of the new city, and force masters to pay fair wages and ensure ongoing work. They could do away with the poor houses. With all the support they had gathered they could see a way forward, for the first time, with their petition to Parliament – making the people who created the wealth, actually share it.

"Abμt 5,000 moiners 'r on straik et th neeow. Thah demanding a peey rise, en eight uhr deey, free cowl te bay peeyed en cash en that feev neets wark should bay peeyed as six deeys."

"I'd like to go back some time to Hanley, John. Jimmy mentioned the Chartists would be speaking again soon. Do you think it is possible we could attend one of those meetings?"

"Way'll say, ducky. Say ef way con wark a dee whan thar's a speech en way con git tarm ef."

CHAPTER 8

Everything had gone a bit quiet in Hanley. There was an uneasy peace but tension remained high. The military pressure, added to the now lengthy strike, began to weaken the will of the striking miners and, by the beginning of August, a partial return to work was underway, with the colliery owners promising to look at the men's grievances. The wandering bands of men, demanding money with threats of violence, began to disperse. However, there were no forthcoming concessions from the pit-owners. It wasn't until the morning of Sunday 7th August when John appeared with more news.

He'd heard that there had been a new turnout at two pits and trouble in Burslem. Three miners, begging for money and food, using a box in Burslem market, were arrested for vagrancy yesterday, and had been locked up under Burslem Town Hall. The word had spread and other miners had decided to free the men. At around midnight a crowd of two hundred attacked the lock up, freeing the three miners and others incarcerated with them, carrying off their friends in triumph. They broke the windows of the police superintendent's house as well as those of the publican, who had been responsible for the arrest. One of the mob, George

Colclough, known locally as Cogsey Nelly, along with a companion, climbed the Town Hall tower and broke the illuminated transparent dial face of the new clock, of which the Burslem Market Trustees were immensely proud, and have since put up an award of £20 for the capture of those responsible. It seems the mob retired before dawn, without being known or identified.

http://www.healeyhero.co.uk/rescue/reminise/rioters.jpg
An engraving from the Illustrated London News of
1842 - showing a picture of the Staffordshire colliers with
whom the 1842 riots were thought to originate

John had also heard that guns and pikes were being sold at secret meetings and that there was even, in some areas, night-time drilling with arms, preparing for the war to come.

Radical newspapers and books were easily obtainable and I noted in one an advertisement for a drink called "The Chartist Beverage", distributed by local teetotal Chartists, who bought quantities of up to one hundred and twenty pounds a week of it from Thomas Cooper. The beverage was in fact a coffee substitute, as real coffee was too expensive for the ordinary working man. In North Staffordshire there was also an active Women's Chartist Movement. They had their own meetings and were known as the 'Female National Charter Association of Upper Hanley and Smallthorne'. The main appeal of the women's movement was to persuade men that women were equally deserving of the vote. Much the same arguments were put forward for women receiving the vote as for men. Their most prominent moment locally was on the visit of Feargus O'Connor to the Potteries. About three hundred of them, along with a band, marched through Lane End to Hanley, each carrying a white wand. Feargus O'Connor spoke of his visit as a "glorious gathering". Chartists had been encouraging men to apply for poor relief, making the system virtually unworkable. In late July 1842, the Burslem and Stoke workhouses were receiving four to five hundred new applications for assistance each day. The Trustees began to complain of Chartist involvement and, although some of this could be due to Chartist encouragement, much, I could see for myself, was due to real need. In early August, Capper, Ellis and John Richards addressed 8 crowds in Hanley, whilst processions of men on outdoor relief marched past. The Chartists felt that now was the time to give working men the chance to run their own lives. They believed that, if they could develop influence, then they would be able to affect foreign policy, which determined export trade, the life blood of the new cities, and force masters to pay fair wages and ensure ongoing work. They could do away with the poor houses and all the social stigmas that 1840s Britain subjected them to. Best of all, as they saw it, for the first time, the people who created the wealth could actually share in it.

I went out to speak to John. "Are there any Chartist meetings planned soon, John? I know it's getting a bit rowdy down there but I'm sure, if you're with me, I'll come to no harm."

"Eet's th'anniverary o' th Peterloo Massacre an Tuesday 16th August but way'll bay warking. Staiks 'r neow an al'over West Midlands en th' North as well as Shropshire en Cheshire. Th Charteest wonna cawl a national 'olideey fer th'anniversary. Eet's lookin' fair dangerous." **(Note 4)**

"But I must go."

"Efun yer say yer moss gay, than yer moss en ah'll bay thar wi' yer nay feeah. Donna flusker yersen."

I gathered from that that I wasn't to get myself overwrought, John would be with me to protect me.

"Cooper's spayking next Sondaay, 14th though. Way con gay than, ef thut's gud."

"Yes, thank you, John. I'd love to hear one of his speeches."

I really had to go, even if it might be dangerous. Otherwise I might miss out on an opportunity to get back to my own time. No matter what, I had to be there. Oh, I did hope that this would be it. I couldn't stand one minute longer with Mr Meigh. I couldn't bear to look at him and I was naturally scared of him. There was no knowing what he would do next.

The Staffordshire Advertiser for 13th August reported on the incident of the box. "The perpetrators of these wanton outrages are believed to consist principally of the more disaffected turn-out colliers, instigated, there is but little doubt, by the Chartists". The report continued saying that, when troops, who had arrived a day later, left the area, a mob of one hundred and fifty went immediately to the police station and demanded the return of the box the men had been using. They then continued soliciting contributions from the inhabitants of the town.

CHAPTER 9

Sunday, 14th August came and John and I were about to make our way to Hanley. I hadn't actually been there before, in this time, as we'd bypassed it on our way to Tufnell. However, on passing the kitchen I saw, on the table, a newspaper heading that caught my eye. It was 'The Guardian' from yesterday. It characterised the workers as a lawless mob. Strike leaders were portrayed as dirty, cowardly and treacherous. In London, the Home Secretary, Sir James Graham, had readied artillery and troops and despatched them toward Lancashire yesterday. On this same day, Queen Victoria issued an edict declaring the illegality of the strikes and offering a £50 reward for turning in a fellow striker.

That was a lot of money, the miners being on a pittance, probably about £5 a month or less, and that was when they were working. I couldn't see this offer being taken up though, the cause was too great, and, as for being dirty, cowardly and treacherous, yes, they were dirty because there was no running water in the hovels they lived in. They definitely weren't cowardly and they were only treacherous because they were fighting the government for rights to live. I was annoyed - stupid, biased, misinformed, Tory newspaper!

John added that things had got so bad with the miners

and potters being out of work that most had sold everything they could or pawned their belongings to turn into money. Jimmy and his family were becoming more and more distressed. They'd sold the beds and what little furniture they had just to buy some food. They were sleeping on the bare floor, covered in coats. "Ah'm geeving 'em what ah con spare." I felt extremely distressed for them but there was nothing I could do because what little money I'd earned, I'd had to buy necessities for myself, having been put here in this time just with the clothes I found myself wearing.

Anyway, we started up the Bank towards Hanley. It was a hot summer's day. John took me on a tour. I thought Tufnell was bad enough but the smell that greeted me was atrocious. It wasn't just the lingering suffocating smoke from the numerous bottle banks (even though most were closed down) that had covered all the buildings in a black slime but the stink of effluence and basically, shit! The gutters were clogged with all sorted of refuse. Water and slops from the houses added to this mess, while the stench from the open drains, outdoor lavatories, in unpaved areas at the back of houses, and cesspools befouled the air. Every little alleyway was basically used as a toilet. John said a sewer had actually been installed, running from the town hall in Fountain Square down to the Fowlea Brook, but this just meant that this brook, which ran around Hanley, was like a moat filled with decomposing filth. John also pointed out the areas that's where the prostitutes plied their trade or thieves hung around waiting for an opportunity to pick a pocket. At night and added that Hanley wasn't a place to go abroad at night, as that's when the thieves plied their trade. Even though the potteries wouldn't be working at night, the stench didn't abate because that was when the night soil cart would come round, removing the human excretion from the closets of each house (of course he didn't use this term but more the vernacular). I asked John where this night soil was taken, not really expecting there to be some sort of sewerage works but that it would most probably be added to the filthy moat around Hanley or possibly big pits, filled in and covered, at intervals, and re-dug in rotation, but he replied that it was mostly used by farmers on their fields, as manure, although no-one had seen any improvement to their crops - so the crops for human consumption were growing up through human shit! – UGH!

Apart from that, Chapel Fields area was fever-ridden, and no-one living there had managed to reach old age. No wonder. The areas of Far Green, Chell Street and the area around Bryan Street had open ditches behind the houses. The Marsh Street area was disease-ridden. The 'Royal' group of streets, so called from their high-sounding names, between Broad Street and Cannon Street, were noted for poverty, filth and crime. The streets north of St. Mark's were also very unhealthy. Etruria suffered from a low-lying situation, a ditch at the back of the houses on one side of the main street and lack of drainage, while in Mill Street (now Etruria Road) the side-walks and channels were in a very poor state and there were open middens in the courts, draining into the street passage.

John showed me where Job Meigh used to have his pottery works. The works included transfer printed and enamelled ware, china and ironstone china. It was now in the hands of Ridgway, Morley, Wear and Company. This area is now a car park at the end of Huntsbach Street, off Town Road. The street is actually called Meigh Street!

There were stocks and a lock-up, or as John said,

'Stonnus' in Trinity Street. In Market Square there was the 'Swan Inn' and the 'French Horn' pub in Fountain Square.

The Hanley I saw was an irregular layout – basically a lot of little island sites, forming an 18th century village. My present day Hanley had been built onto this and Hanley now has buildings of widely different heights, styles and materials. Of course, the 'INTU Potteries' shopping city wasn't there or any other little shops in Town Road. The classical style buildings containing the Weatherspoon's pub 'The Reginald Mitchell' and 'Waterstones' were there but at this time were a butchers slaughterhouse with a cattle market nearby in Lower Bethesda Street. There were a few low-built brick houses in New Hall Street, Parliament Road and Tontine Street, still standing from the early 19th century. On the south side of Fountain Square the 'French Horn' public house and present day adjoining shops were low-built brick houses. In New Hall Street the Georgian front of Hope Congregational Church was there, little changed from today. The buildings in parts of Pall Mall, Albion Street and Bagnall Street seemed to retain something of the scale of the early town. Bathesda Chapel was there but had obviously been altered later on. To the south of St. Mark's Church there were some middle-class terraces houses and several larger houses in their own gardens. Some of these, I noted, are still standing in present day.

The Neo-Classical parish church of St John the Evangelist was there on the corner of Town Road (which I noted was now called the High Street) and Quadrant Road, in all its glory, with its decorative gallery columns, window frames and castellations. This particular church had, unfortunately, stood derelict for many years in the 20/21st centuries but now this Grade ll listed building has been resurrected but converted into a restaurant, of all things, as they do - either a restaurant or a pub.

I could also see that Hanley had a town hall in Town Road. Of course, this isn't there now, being rebuilt at the far end of Pall Mall. I believe, before that, the town hall was built in impressive classical style on Fountain Square, but Lloyds Bank took it over in the late 19th century.

Of course, there were a great many potbanks around, spewing out smoke – to name a few: Eastwood factory, known as the 'seven sisters', Dudson Pottery, Hope Street; Bell Pottery (junction of Albion Street and Broad Street) but these potbanks stretched into all surrounding areas – Burslem, Etruria, Longton, Bucknall, Tunstall, Stoke, Stanton, et al.

Hanley 19th Century
outlined area is where Job Meigh's factory was

www.thepotteries.org.

Thomas Cooper, self-styled General of the Shakespearean Brigade of Chartists, had arrived in Hanley yesterday, Saturday, 13th August. He'd lodged with Jeremiah Yates, a local distributor of radical publication and Chartist beverage. Yesterday the streets were quiet. Today, he'd been to Fenton and then onto Longton to speak. This evening he was due to speak at the Crown Inn, Hanley, on spare ground called the Crown Bank.

We made our way there. An immense crowd gathered, waving banners with slogans such as "Liberty or Death", "United we stand, divided we fall" and people waving the green, be-starred, Chartist flag and posters put up on walls. Thomas Cooper had put a chair in front of the Crown Inn and stood on it to speak to the crowd. His voice could be heard over the crowd like a peal of a trumpet, even to the far edge of the crowd. "Good morning, friends."

Who stood before us was a man in his mid 30s – dark, wavy hair swept back from his high forehead, to just about his shoulders. His lips were full and red and he would have been handsome if it were not for a small chin. He had eyes that gave the appearance of an energetic man but also passionate and caring; however, these same eyes seemed to be able to penetrate the crowd and mesmerise.

Crown Bank, Hanley Crown Bank is an open area adjacent to Stafford Street - immediately behind is Piccadilly. To the left (off the picture) is Fountain Square. In the centre is Market Lane and off to the right is Percy Street. This area was the centre for the horse drawn cabs.

Buildings
To the left is the Dolphin public house
(The Midland Bank is located on this spot now)
The white building in the centre says:
Established 1840, MILLERS
House Furnishers and Haberdashers

To the right is another public house advertising "Parkers Celebrated Ales"

http://www.thepotteries.org/postcards/hanley/x_crown_bank.jpg

On our way around Hanley, I picked up the following leaflets that were being handed out.

ANTI-BREAD-TAX TRACTS FOR THE PEOPLE

No 3.

Remember: Every dozen lbs of flour you consume pays 9d tax for monopoly. The price is 2s 9d; 2s would be only 1s 6d if there was not a bread tax.

WORKING MEN!

You are told that the masters are tyrants! Is that any reason why you should pay 9d tax on every dozen lbs of flour you or your families eat?

You are told that the masters want to reduce wages when the bread-tax is abolished! Has the bread-tax kept up wages?

You are told that cheap flour means low wages Then the bread-tax has not kept up wages.

You are told that cheap flour means low wages! Flour is selling in America at little more than half our price, and wages there are nearly double yours. Wages are always highest when bread is cheapest.

You are told not to join the middle class in getting a repeal of the bread-tax!

Universal Suffrage

Run the risk of all the consequences of getting three loaves where you now get only two!

You are told that the anti-corn-law men are opposed to Chartism! They are opposed to no party; - their motto is BREADISM and their wish is to benefit all parties.

REMEMBER! EVERY DOZEN LBS OF FLOUR YOU AND YOUR FAMILIES CONSUME PAY A TAX OF 9d FOR MONOPOLY

You are told that we may get the

CHARTER

as soon or sooner than we shall abolish the bread-tax!

Look at facts! One hundred and seventy nine members of the   House of Commons voted in favour of Mr Villiers' motion for going into the question of the corn-law, and forty-six in favour of Mr Attwood's motion for going into the question of the   Charter; hundreds of newspapers advocate the repeal of the corn-law, and four newspapers advocate the Charter.

You are told that something very dreadful may happen if we abolish the bread-tax before you get

> ## *WORKING MEN!*
>
> *Who suffer most from the bread-tax – you or the middle class?*
>
> *You are told that the middle class kept aloof when the working men opposed the bread-tax! The middle class were then wrong and the working class right. Is that a good reason why the working class should now be wrong because the middle class are right?*
>
> *You are told to keep aloof from the anti-corn-law "humbugs!" our pockets cannot keep aloof; you pay 9d tax upon every dozen lbs of flour you and your families eat.*
>
> *You are told to get the Charter first, and repeal the corn-law afterwards! Will you get the Charter any soon by continuing to pay 9d tax upon every dozen lbs of flour you eat?*

First of all he had the crowd sing Bramwich's hymn, "Britannia's sons, though slaves ye be" He had a backing band of fiddles and accordion.

Britannia's sons though slaves ye be
God your creator made you free
He life and thought and being gave
But never ever made a slave

His works are wonderful to see
All all proclaim the deity
He made the earth and formed the waves
But never, never made a slave.

He made the sky with spangles bright
The moon to shine by silent night
The sun – and spread the vast concave
But never, never made a slave.

The verdant earth on which we tread
Was by his hand all carpeted
Enough for all he freely gave
But never, never made a slave.

All men are equal in his sight
The bond, the free, the black, the white
He made them all, then freedom gave
God made the man – Man made the slave.

He started off his speech with the sixth commandment, 'Thou shalt do no murder'.

"Thou shalt do no murder, citizens of Hanley. All through history the ruling classes, the landed gentry have gathered slaves to themselves, to work the land for themselves. From time immemorial there have been slaves – the people of Israel, put into slavery by the Pharaohs of Egypt, to build their pyramids; the slaves brought over from Africa to work the cotton fields and tobacco plantations in America. These slaves are helping to build the new nation into an economic powerhouse but are being deprived of food and freedom. Their owners selling the food stored for their slaves, to line their own pockets, and all the while these slaves getting nothing for their hard work, being sold and bartered in the market-places, the plantation owners raping the women. I speak also of the conquerors of America, who have nearly exterminated the native races, and thus violated the precept,

"Thou shalt do no murder". The same is happening here in Britain. The Dutch, French, Spanish, Portuguese and Arabs all have their slaves.

Pirates from North Africa also captured Europeans sailing in the Mediterranean and made them slaves. They also raided the coastal regions of Spain, Portugal, France, Italy, Ireland and southwest England for slaves. They even sailed as far as Iceland and took the inhabitants as slaves. This white slave trade only ended in the 1830s when the French conquered the region.

Meanwhile from the 15th century to the 18th century, Crimean Tatars raided the Slavic lands to the north for slaves. A vast number of Slavs were captured and most were sold in the Ottoman Empire. The slave trading finally ended in 1783 when Catherine the Great, Empress of Russia captured Crimea.

Also, last century, that Christless man, Clive of India, was exhorted by his peers, for amassing a fortune for himself and the East India Company, while torturing the Indians to disclose their treasures and ransacking cities, towns and villages. Their once prosperous weavers and artisans were put into slavery by their new masters and were starving to death, following the crop failure in Bengal, around 1770. Clive's policies had not included storing food for such emergencies and he, instead, sold off the food that was produced, for yet more money. Clive returned to England as the richest man in Europe. Ye all are suffering the same here. The rich get rich and the poor get poorer.

Remember how the English and French and Spanish and German wars in modern history had swollen the list of the slaughtered and had violated the precept, 'Thou shalt do no murder'. Do ye know that, at the beginning of this century an estimated three-quarters of all people alive were trapped in bondage against their will, either in some form of slavery or selfdom? We must fight to win our freedom. Are ye with me?" he called out to the crowd.

The crowd responded with cheers and stamping their feet, banging on whatever they could to make a noise.

"And who has to pay for these wars, yes, the tax payer, THEE. The immense taxation we had been forced to endure, to enable our rulers to maintain the long and ruinous war with France and Napoleon, has entailed indescribable suffering on millions, and that thus had been violated the precept, 'Thou shalt do no murder'.

Yes, ye are slaves, ye don't call thyselves slaves, ye think ye are free men but ye all are if ye are working for a pittance with not enough to feed your families. Ye are all starving, looking around for a piece of bread, while they live from the fat of the land and sell thy hard-earned produce to others to line their own pockets and leave nothing for the toilers, yes ye toilers, who have broken thy backs to please thy governors, for nothing. There's no bread to feed ye, they've taxed it so high ye cannot afford it and instead sell it abroad. How can ye survive with landowners who leave ye not enough to even feed your families. Ye have got nothing for thy labours. Ye live in hovels and squalor whilst they are building mansions fit for kings – all from thy hard toil. Ye haven't got clothes, ye are in rags, ye do not have thine own house, ye have to pay rent to these landlords, for a dirty fleapit. What do ye get in return? That's right, nothing.

My mother procured me bread by the labour of her own hands; and I have often known her give me the last

bit of food in our humble home, while she herself fasted....
I frequently knew, in childhood, what it was to go shoeless,
and to wear ragged clothing. I am surrounded by starving
men: an experience to which the majority of you are no
strangers. I know your strife, your worries, your fears."

And what do ye get if ye are not fit enough for work
because ye are too weak to work – a good slapping with a
belt or whip, then they throw ye out of thy job and out of
thy houses and ye have to resort to the dreaded workhouses,
run by so-called Christian ministers. That's the end of the
road for ye – there's no way out and, if ye try to escape, ye
are cruelly beaten. Thy families are split up, thy identity
is taken away from ye, ye are fed on meagre rations of
gruel, not enough to sustain a body, and submitted to hard
labour – nothing more than a prison where ye'll probably
die of starvation and sickness anyway.

This all violates the sixth commandment – 'Thou shalt
not do murder'. These landowners are committing murder
and getting away with it."

Boos and hisses went up from the crowd.

"As ye know, there used to be parish assistance for the
poor in our land but this was repealed in 1834 by the Poor
Law Amendment Act. The greedy landowners decided they
no longer wanted to give money to the parishes and to
ensure that workhouses were worse than the conditions of
the independent labourer. This Act also forbade the keeping
of pigs and poultry for your own personal needs, so adding
to each family's hardships in times of famine. I know the
hardships ye are all suffering and that many of you will soon
have no other means than to apply to the Poor Houses for
assistance. I assert herewith, that you should all apply. By

doing so ye will break the backs of the Poor Houses and thus this atrocious Poor Law Act will have to be repealed."

There was a lot of mumbling in the crowds about this.

"I assert also that the imposition of the Bread Tax was a violation of the same precept; and that such was the enactment of the Game Laws; that such was the custom of primogeniture and keeping of land in the possession of the privileged classes; and that such was the enactment of infamous new Poor Law."

The general murmur of applause now began to swell into loud cries; and these were mingled with execrations of the authors of the poor Law.

"Across the North, the Midlands and indeed the Potteries, my friends, many workers have been unemployed or on strike for most of the summer, and we have been frustrated by the refusal of parliament to consider the second presentation of the Charter that happened in May. Despite the more than three million signatures on the petition, ten thousand of those signatures coming from thy district of North Staffordshire, it failed even to win a hearing, by a vote of 287 to 46. This is out of order but we are not beaten. We will be presenting the Charter again – and this time it will be heard. We WILL get our rights heard"

A loud cheer went up from the audience.

Yes, three and a half million of the slave-class have holden out the olive branch of peace to the enfranchised and privileged classes and sought for a firm and compact union, on the principle of EQUALITY BEFORE THE LAW; and the enfranchised and privileged have refused to enter into a treaty! The same class is to be a slave class still. The mark and brand of inferiority is not to be removed. The assumption of inferiority is still to be maintained. They declare in so doing that the people are not to be free.

But we are not going to let this happen. We are not going to give up the fight. This is what I declare - 'It will be an easy matter to get the Charter, for if only one-tenth part of the population came out on a certain day, the enfranchised and privileged will not succeed. I ague that, by withholding labour, workers can eliminate the aristocracy, monarchy and the church. The High lords and kings must cease to sit in pride – without thy toil. There will be a tide of retribution against these wolves in sheep's clothing till ye end the game. In addition to their unearned profit siphoned off the labour of the poor, priests "proclaim content" and counsel passive resignation to the oppressed. Significantly, the destruction of this trinity of oppression occurs not through bloodshed but rather through peaceful transformation as it appears in The Purgatory of Suicides.

We shall all have the Charter and nothing can stop us. There are not ten soldiers for every town in the kingdom to hold us back."

There were nods and murmurs around the crowd to this statement. I got the impression that it hadn't dawned on them until hearing Cooper's speech, that there were so few soldiers to stand up against.

Someone in the crowd spoke up high above the murmuring and skuffle. "How 'r way warkers gonna bay able te survaive eff in way eliminate the masters, ef way com owt on straik?"

Cooper answered, "I answer you thus. Why, how do they live elsewhere? They DO live, but perhaps not very well, and yet almost as well as the poor working people. Ye must not forget ye have the fields full of food, but I don't tell ye to steal it. I do not say I would steal it myself, and therefore would not advise ye to do what I was not willing to do myself; but there it is, and this is not a world in which people should starve.

Why do ye dig, slave and suffer to glut the tyrant-forgers of your chain?"

Cooper then read one of his own poems:
"Slaves, toil no more! Up, from the midnight mine,
   Summon your swarthy thousands to the plain
Beneath the bright sun marshalled, swell the strain
   Of Liberty; and, while the lordlings view
Your banded hosts, with stricken heart and brain,
   Shout, as one man,-- 'Toil we no more renew,
Until the Many cease their slavery to the Few!'

He continued. "Miners, I urge you to move up from darkness to light – turn from ignorance to consciousness. Please sing with me the Hymn to Liberty.

Great God! Is this the Patriot's doom?
Shall they who dare defend the slave,
Be Hur'ld within a prison's gloom
To fit them for an early grave?

Shall victim after victim fall,
A prey to cruel class-made laws?
Forbid it Lord! On Thee we call,
Protect us and defend our cause.

In vain we pray'd the powers that be
To burst the drooping captive's chain,
But mercy, Lord, belongs to Thee,
For thou has freed him from all pain.

Is this the price of Liberty?
Must Martyr's fall to gain the prize?
Then be it so! We will be free,
Or all become a sacrifice!
Tho' Freedom mourns her murder's son,
And weeping friends surround his bier;
Tho' tears like mountain torrents run,
Our cause is water'd by each tear."

After the song, Cooper requested the crowd to fold their hands in a gesture that mimicked prayer but also indicated an abstinence from work.

"Join but to fold your hands, and ye will foil
To utter helplessness,--yea, to the core
Strike both their power and craft with
death! Slaves, toil no more!"

Joseph Capper addressed the meeting. "I urge ye to seek thy rights, but by peaceful means."

As Cooper stood down from his chair he announced that he would be addressing another meeting, primarily of striking colliers at 9am the next day."

Cooper then retired for the night.

I was bemused as to what my involvement would be in Hanley. Yes, I was intrigued as I was witnessing history in the making, and wanted to see the outcome, but obviously a little worried…. but then again, I wanted to hear the Chartists speak, hear what they had to say. Still, I'd made up my mind.

"E's probably goin' te The George en Dragon Inn" said John. Eets thah 'eadquarters".

The meeting then broke up, but there was a great deal of murmuring in the crowd, raised words, arguments. The crowd was still inflamed from Cooper's speech yesterday.

"John, Thomas Cooper said he'd be speaking again tomorrow at 9am. I really want to be here to see the outcome. Trouble is, we're both supposed to be working. How can we do this?"

"Donna fear, ducky. Th Masters gonna be involved in all ef thayse dimonstrations, ay'l bay owt wi' th'uther mageestrates. 'E won't bay at hame. Way con snake away. Tell Mistress you're not well, or ev te viseet yer ma, or someet."

We made our way to the George and Dragon Inn.

As we walked there, I considered Cooper's speech. He really drove home the plight of the potters and miners. As for them being slaves – well, they were free to leave, but where could they go to when every other pot or colliery-owner were of like mind on the abysmal way they treated their workers. The workers had no rights, there were no unions. If they didn't work for the pittance that kept them on starvation rations, they didn't work at all and found themselves in the Poor House, where they'd probably die. There was no way out but to strike.

My mind then wandered back to my own time. Slavery hadn't been abolished and was still flourishing. Women forced into prostitution. People forced to work in agriculture, domestic work and factories. Children in sweatshops producing goods sold globally. Entire families forced to work for nothing to pay off generational debts. Girls forced to marry older men. This isn't just something happening in far off countries but is rife in the UK. Slavery has been legally abolished but is now under the radar.

Also, I thought about these zero hour contracts jobs that had been set up, in my time, where the employer is not obliged to provide any minimum working hours, while the worker is, supposedly, not obliged to accept any work offered, or so the agreement goes! The employee may sign an agreement to be available for work as and when required, so that no particular number of hours of work are specified. That wasn't working as, basically, the employee wasn't guaranteed any work, and certainly not enough to live on – no holiday pay, no sickness benefits, no National Insurance pension payments and just left waiting on the end of a phone for a few hours work at any time of day or night, which they have to accept, otherwise they wouldn't have enough to eat or pay their bills - while the employer is getting cheap labour, only if vitally needed and only have to pay the minimum wage at that. It was a racket. So, nothing had changed from the past in that respect.

We found Thomas Cooper there with other Chartist speakers.

As John had said, The George and Dragon was a popular meeting place for the Chartists and unofficial headquarters of the local Chartist committee

Cooper took the stage.

"Friends, I have news from Manchester. As ye know, our northern comrades have been on strike and workers turned out from factories with 2,000 workers marching through the streets in a peaceful demonstration of strength. At the end of July, factory masters in the Ashton-Stalybridge area, south-east of Manchester, announced a twenty-five per cent reduction in wages. On 26th July, a large public meeting was chaired by William Woodruffe, our Ashton Chartist delegate, with two main speakers, William Aitken and Richard Pilling, with another meeting at Stalybridge on 29th July. Both meetings called for arms to be raised to protect the working classes. Further meetings were held over the next few days in Hyde and Dukinfield. However, on Sunday, 7th August, a large Chartist meeting was held at Mottram Moor, where resolutions were carried in support of a strike for a fair day's pay, and the Charter, and it was announced that there would be a general turn-out throughout Lancashire and Cheshire the following morning. Richard Pilling, a weaver from Ashton, led a party from Ashton to Oldham to spread the strike, and the following day the strikers were ready to march on Manchester. This was a peaceful rally and most factories turned-out with little or no violence, although there was some military resistance at the Birley Mills in Oxford Street but by Saturday, 13th August, Birley's too was forced to close.

This turn-out, comrades, has now spread northwards and eastwards to Rochdale and Bolton and over the Pennines to Halifax. Every factory within fifty miles of Manchester has now been closed, spreading to Scotland and West Yorkshire. Workers have been marching for the cause. There have been trade conferences in each city debating the crucial question of whether to steer the strike firmly towards presenting our Charter to parliament or to remain narrowly focused on wages issues.

This, my friends, has worried the Home Secretary, for good reason as, what has come out of it is the Great Delegate Conference in Manchester, chaired by the Chartist, Alexander Hutchinson, who is secretary of the Manchester smiths and a member of the NCA executive. On 11th August, this conference with delegates from various industries including mechanics, engineers, millwrights, moulders and smiths, met to agree a common programme of action.

As ye know, O'Connor had been reticent to support the strikes, seeing them both as an Anti-Corn Law League plot and as a trap to discredit us Chartists. We are diametrically opposed to the Anti-Corn Law League as they advocate exploiting working class disorder, which we Chartists are against. However, we are now committed and I have to report, my friends, that I have great news – the Great Delegate Conference in Manchester has OVERWHELMINGLY voted to ENDORSE both the Charter and a return to 1840 wage rates, and to **cease work** until the Charter becomes the law of the land – up to half a million people are now **on strike** with local committees being put in place to direct the strikes."

A great cheer went up.

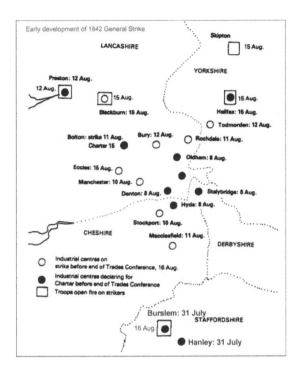

http://www.thepotteries.org/chartism/general strike.jpg

From what I understood, these northern manufacturers were causing strikes and agitation to unsettle a government they disliked. An Anti-Corn Law League was formed, which largely represented the free-trade mill- and factory-owners – to discredit the Chartist movement and apply pressure to the trade protectionist government. In fact, the first strikes had started on Sunday the 7th of August in Lancashire in response to Anti-Corn Law manufacturers reducing wages

Cooper continued, "We will be meeting here again tomorrow but, in the meantime, I will close the meeting with a hymn to commend our Chartist leader Feargus O'Connor, who has been imprisoned for our cause, for liberty for the people, but is continuing to write for the Northern Star:

> "The Lion of Freedom is come from his den;
> We'll rally around him, again and again;
> We'll crown him with laurel, our champion to be;
> O'Connor, the patriot, for sweet Liberty!

CHAPTER 10

The next morning, 15th August 1842, John and I made our way to The Crown Bank, Hanley again. As John had predicted, Job Meigh wasn't present and I told Mrs Meigh that I had to visit a sick relative in Leek but assured her I would be back that evening. She wasn't happy, a bit distressed, but I didn't belong there anyway. If I lost my job, that wouldn't be any hardship as I'd be able to get away from Job Meigh. This was more important. I had to try to get my way back to my own time.

Thomas Cooper and other Chartist speakers were there - William Ellis and John Richards, who looked about 70 years of age. There was a huge crowd that I reckoned was in the region of eight to ten thousand. The meeting started with the Chartist Hymn No. 5:

> Men of England, ye are slaves,
> Bought by tyrants, sold by knaves;
> Your's the toil, the sweat, the pain,
> Their's the profit, ease, and gain.

> Men of England, ye are slaves;
> Beaten by policemen's staves;

> If their force ye dar repel,
> Yours will be the felon's cell.
>
> Men of England, ye are slaves;
> Hark! The stormy tempest raves
> 'Tis the nation's voice I hear
> Shouting, "Liberty is near!".

Thomas Cooper stood on his chair to address the crowd with his booming voice. "I wish firstly to appoint myself, Thomas Cooper, the chairman of the meeting.

Just in case some of you did not hear my speech yesterday. I am pleased to announce that the Great Delegate Conference in Manchester has endorsed our Charter and return to 1840 wage rates." We are to **cease work** until the Charter becomes the law of the land."

A cheer went up.

"They stated, and I read herewith: We the delegates representing the various trades of Manchester and its vicinities, with delegates from various parts of Lancashire and Yorkshire, do most emphatically declare that it is our solemn and conscientious conviction that all the evils that afflict society, and which have prostrated the energies of the great body of the producing classes, arise solely from class legislation; and that the only remedy for the present alarming distress and widespread destitution is the immediate and unmutilated adoption and carrying into law, the document known as the Peoples' Charter."

Thomas Cooper raised his head from the paper and scanned the crowd with his piercing eyes. He loudly proclaimed, "This means that we can proceed with the presentation of the People's Charter to Parliament. We can present our requests for:

1. Suffrage for all able-minded men over 21 years of age – that means the vote for all adult men.
2. That each Member of Parliament represent the same number of electors, to present unequal representation.
3. That all men be eligible for Parliament, without a property qualification – that means all men can apply to be a Member of Parliament, if they so wish, to decide the rights and laws of this land, without having to own their own property.
4. A secret ballot, to protect electors. This is to do away with the present show of hands voting, so there will be no discrimination by employers who have, in the past, laid off men if they are seen to be voting against their wishes.
5. Annual elections for Parliament, to ensure accountability and limit bribery.
6. Payment of Members of Parliament, to enable the poor or middle-class serve."

The meeting proposed appointing delegates to wait upon and confer with shopkeepers, dissenting clergymen and the middle classed generally for the purpose of ascertaining how far they are prepared to assist and support the people in the struggle for the attainment of their political right. "I propose that John Richards should go to the Manchester convention as the Potteries delegate." This was seconded. "I also propose that there should be a meeting here tomorrow, Tuesday, at 6am." This was agreed by those present.

He continued, "If ye support this resolution, no government on earth can resist our demands. However, I insist that peace, law and order must be thy motto. And if ye keep thy strike peaceful, ye have nothing to fear from the law."

Joseph Capper also addressed the meeting, "I urge ye all to seek thy right, but by peaceable means. It is the opinion of this meeting that nothing but the People's Charter can give us the power to have a fair day's wage for a fair day's work."

John Richards proposed the resolution. "All labour must cease until the People's Charter becomes the law." This was seconded. All in favour raise your hands

There was an immediate raising of hands throughout the crowd and cheering.

Cooper took the stand "We decree that, with the resolution, all labour should cease, ye shall strike until the people's Charter becomes the law of the land."

The ambiguity of the word 'strike', having the two meanings - hit and to cease labour - had been stressed throughout Cooper's speech yesterday - and the crowd were aware of this. They had been well and truly roused up. They weren't just going to go quietly. There was a lot of pushing and shoving and banter going on. Some began to leave, others stayed.

I heard people shouting out, "Revenge", "Mek 'em peeay", "Way've 'ad enough" Just behind me I heard someone shout out. "Follah may." Then a great cheer went up all round and the crowd started to move across the Crown Bank. There was fire in their eyes and souls. I heard someone shout out, "ay wants us te straik, well way're gonna but no' payceful loik ay wants." This was taken up by the crowd, "Straik, straik, straik". They were out for vengeance and forty or fifty of the audience left. John and I decided to follow them, trying to keep our distance. John held onto my arm, not necessarily for protection but to keep me close, as the mass of the screaming crowd was pushing and shoving and more joined on behind us. Surely I wasn't meant to join this mad marauding crowd in order to be able to return to my own time. I was a little worried…. scrap that thought, I said to myself… I was scared that it was such a dangerous place to be at this time and I could get hurt or even killed. But I couldn't not be there - if we kept our distance…..

In their madness they were merciless even to men of their own order. They went straight to Earl Granville's Shelton colliery, raked out the fire and pulled the plugs of the engines. The mob charged up the street shouting, "to the lock up! Release the prisoners!"

We followed them to Longton and their numbers were increasing all the time.

Longton in my day is a hive of industrial activity, not really a nice area, as such, because of the factories and workshops. What I saw, on entering the area though, after passing by fields and open areas, which are now all built on, should have been expected. Longton was an unplanned mismatch of old hamlet houses and commercial properties - lots of potbanks, as ever, plus coal mines, and the sludge and sewerage of Hanley, but there was public lighting! There were the usual open privies, with cesspools overflowing onto the pavement, refuse in heaps; puddles (probably urine as they'd been no rain). There didn't seem to be any drainage from the privies and there were heaps of ash from the fires and cooking stoves in the little houses, some of which stood six feet above the level of the house doors. I'm saying 'houses' but some of these were little more than miserable, single-roomed, windowless huts for a whole family of parents and God knows how many children.

John said he'd actually gone into one of these houses, having met a guy in a pub and been invited back for 'one for the road' and he'd seen refuse being thrown into the cellar, which was also waterlogged. He hadn't seen any facilities for running water. It was a horrible area and time to live, as a family home was often surrounded by detritus, with no provision for drainage or cleansing. The men would come back from a day's work to a stinking home, not able to wash, and just go down the pub, and John presumed that this was the normal way of living in this neighbourhood, not just this household. It was also the habit of the pit and bottle-bank owners to pay the wages to the landlord of the nearest pub. This meant the workers had to go to the pub to collect their wages. The unscrupulous landlords would make them pay for a pie out of their wages, and, of course, the men would stay for a few pints, or more, and finally arrive home, blind drunk and virtually penniless, again.

They were living like the pigs I saw in sties scattered around - living in their own dirt. Of course, John added, this was before the new Poor Law Act came about, disallowing the keeping of pigs and poultry for a family's own needs. This was no life, especially for the women. John got out of this house he visited as soon as he could, as there was no welcome for him and the wife, through the neglect and drunken habits of her husband, had become hardened and bitter, shouting at whoever, berating her husband and screaming at the kids. The children were dirty, hard-faced urchins and, with no good examples to live up to, had become dangerous hooligans, ready to fight, kick and torment anyone who came near them or their territory.

Anyway, we continued to follow the mob. At the police station they soon freed the half dozen inmates, armed themselves with clubs kept for the special constables and proceeded to break up the furniture and smash the windows. We could see papers being thrown out of windows and set fire to. By now there were about two hundred men and boys in the mob. An open-air meeting then took place. We were too far away to hear but, as soon as this was over, the mob broke into a wild havoc. Shops were broken open and their contents thrown out to the hungry crowd. Indiscriminate plunder was thus pursued among unoffending people. They set on pawn brokers in the area and the owners were so intimidated that they were getting objects from their shops and handing them over to the mob. That wasn't enough for the mob and they just entered the shops and took what they wanted.

The mob continued onto Mr Gibbs, the Poor Rate collector, who in their minds had been the cause of so much misery, and destroyed his books. Not just that but they then threw his cage birds on the ground and trampled them underfoot. This was extremely distressing for me to watch but I couldn't do anything about it. The mob wasn't just out of control, they were out for murder. It seemed that anything or anyone to do with the police, poor law, or debtor's court were to be laid waste.

They fell on the Court of Requests at Shelton, destroying

books and papers and furniture, and violently attacked the clerk.

Now they headed towards Stoke where they immediately headed for the police station. The police here appeared to have been forewarned and had secured the windows and doors. They soon broke in, over-powered the police and tried to burn down their office. Men from the mob were coming out of the police station, having armed themselves with cutlasses taken from the police station. A policeman was screaming that his arm was broken – but I saw that he managed to get away, and I saw someone else, not in uniform, being struck down by a cutlass. A shout went out "Stonier, the chief, 'as escaped, the yellow, cowardly bugger, 'es run orf en left 'is woif!" This followed by a few other swear words. This man dragged Stonier's wife out onto the street. She was carrying a cat. The man grabbed the cat out of her arms and, to my horror, cut off the cat's head. "You're next missus." He screamed. Fortunately the wife manged to wrangle free and ran upstairs, presumably locking herself in. "Aw, leave har" said another man. "Shay's no' worth eet. Shay's not oor problem, let's gay."

From here the crowd rushed onto Fenton and headed towards a particular house. I heard, "Mr Allen's place 'as got weapons – don't the militia store them thar?" They kicked the door down but there were disgruntled looks of the men coming back out. They'd found nothing much, just a brace of pistols and a sword.

The military came upon this scene of destructive fury and there was a fierce conflict between them and the rioters. The military managed to halt the rioting for the time being by arresting the ringleaders. The mob split into two. One group went off in the direction of Penkhull.

John and I decided not to follow the crowd any more, we didn't want to get mixed up with the arresting military, so we decided to head back to the 'George and Dragon'.

On the way we came across a large meeting of colliers at Ridgway's coal mine. The meeting seemed to be quiet and contained so we stopped a while to listen. Here Mr Ridgway was holding a meeting of his own to hear about the workers' grievances and counsel moderation. I remember John telling me he was one of the few fair pit owners, paying fair wages, looking after the welfare of the sick under his charge. Just then Sneyd, a local magistrate and coal owner approached at the head of cavalry and infantry, telling the crowd to disperse, as per his orders. Mr Ridgway requested the right to continue the meeting but Sneyd ignored this request and read the Riot Act. There was uproar now amongst the crowd. They hadn't been doing any harm and were not out of order, just listening to their boss' counsel. Sneyd, wasn't going to allow any crowd meetings, no matter how calm and controlled and sent the infantry forward to arrest all in the crowd.

"John, run, quick…. let's get out of here". I screamed at him. So we ran as fast as possible in the direction of Hanley.

Safely back at the 'George and Dragon', more information was coming in about the day's riots and some of the drunken rioters had made their way to the pub revelling in the destruction they'd carried out. In Hanley another attack had been made upon the parsonage of the Rev. R E Aitkins. Here, unfortunately, more beer and wines were found, and the desperate men who drank them were ready for any villainy. This house was set on fire and its contents destroyed. From this house they went to Lawyer Parker's, and his house was soon wrapped in flames. It seems the mob we saw moving in the direction of Penkhull had gone on to try to destroy the Stoke workhouse, but could not gain entry, so they went to the house of Mr Bailey Rose, the stipendiary magistrate, who was out leading the infantry we had just seen. They had completely gutted his house by fire. The other half of the mob had gone onto Longton. By half past one in the afternoon there were several thousand people gathered near the Town Hall in Longton. They started breaking the windows of that building, and moved onto the Police Station and the Parish Office. Houses were attacked in a similar vein, but inn-keepers were more fortunate. They bribed the rioters with free drink for not damaging their hostelries. Some householders paid the mob to leave them be.

When the mob arrived at the house of the rector of Longton, Dr Vale, at about 2pm their activities were, at first, moderated by the presence of his wife, but the discovery of the rector's cellars had a contrary effect: 'crowds of females manifested the greatest eagerness to partake among others of the liquor'. They were seen carrying alcohol, which a man had brought from the cellar, in a pint basin, and saying to her companions, "'ere wenches, drink. Thah's plentah more." The mob had got themselves so drunk they could not stand to run away. One woman was fortunate to escape by being placed in a wheelbarrow by friends and removed. Those in hearing distance in the pub all had a good laugh at that, all having imbibed well themselves.

The rector's furniture and his valuable collection of rare

books fuelled a bonfire. Furniture was thrown out of the windows onto a fire in front of the house. Someone was seen demolishing the woodwork around the windows while others were seen breaking bedroom furniture by banging the pieces together. and the house itself also was ignited. Someone, who hearing this, remarked, "ay well deserved eet. Eet was 'im who'd mayed the crass remark about 'ow way poor people should use grass and leaves te mek tay ef way conna afford to bay it fer th' shops. Good reedance t'im, thut's what ah says."

It seems, saying Dr Vale was not well liked, was an understatement!

Anyway, Mr Dawes, the surgeon, arrived with a fire engine, followed by the 2nd Dragoons, and not only saved the structure but converted some who had hitherto been passive spectators into active defenders of Dr Vale's property. Prisoners were taken and conducted to Newcastle for imprisonment.

The original man continued, reporting that the mob then went to Trentham Police House. This, too, was gutted by fire but the Leveson-Gowers were more fortunate. They had kept about sixty of their estate men to guard the property all night. The Leveson-Gowers were not going to trust their immense assets to the local police force or yeomanry, but then they were big enough to make their own provision. In the event, the mob decided to return to Hanley.

Another said he'd seen one rioter, a twenty nine year old, called Thomas Adkins, being arrested and he'd heard he'd been taken to Newcastle for imprisonment and died there this afternoon. He didn't know if this man had been beaten up by the police or what, but he was dead. A hush fell on the pub on hearing this. The riots had claimed their first victim.

Cooper went out into the streets to see for himself and observed shopkeepers shutting up shop and driving off in their gigs. By 5pm some of the rioters had come back to the pub and, by 6pm, the crowd was so large, consisting of thousands, all assembling for Cooper's evening address, due to start at 8pm. Some of the men were pushing through to try to shake hands with Cooper. I could see that Cooper looked extremely annoyed and pushed these outstretched hands aside. I heard someone from the committee suggest to Cooper that he had better begin talking at 7pm.

Thomas Cooper took to the stage again.

"Before I begin, some of you men have gotten yourselves into drunken states. I am ashamed of this depravity. I understand there has been mayhem, theft and violence with many buildings wrecked."

I had seen earlier a company of infantry marching by, bayonets fixed, on their way to Longton, along with two magistrates. I believe they were the 12th Company, with Parker and Bailey Rose as the magistrates, going to disrupt the malicious mob out for vengeance and to bring order.

"I do not commend thee for thy depredations, and most strongly reprove thee for thy drunkenness. In my speeches I forswore against violence of any sort. No doubt my passionate declamations have been misunderstood, but ye have caused wild destruction. I never willingly suggested such. Anyone who has participated in these acts of violence and destruction of property can no longer call themselves our friends, but the enemies of freedom – that ruin to themselves and others must attend this strike for the Charter if they who pretended to be its advocates broke the law."

Of course his speeches would lead to riots, I thought to myself. No matter what he said about acting in accordance with the law, he'd instilled the crowd to violence with his speeches and songs such as the 'Lion of Freedom' song. To desperate men, these weren't just words, they were a life line, they were a call to rise up and overthrow the suppressors – he was using language which could only lead to one result and someone had already died with many injured. What else did he expect!

Cooper took a pause to regain his demeanour. He raised his head and hands to the crowd. "I congratulate those who have freed the imprisoned miners in Burslem earlier" and pointed to Cogsey Nelly, who was in the crowd." A cheer went up. "Our cause must be patriotic and noble of purpose. Ye oppressed sons of toil, the country we live in is a great hypocrite, for while it pretends to be a hater of slavery in other lands, the rich enslave the poor by tens of thousands. Slaves, toil no more, but in your thousands go and tame the proud. We must strike, but I insist it must be a peaceful and legal process."

At dusk the meeting drew to a close but the people weren't leaving. Suddenly two pistol shots rang out. Cooper shouted out to the crowd to call a policeman but is seems no policemen were in the vicinity – no-one came. There was no sign of anyone in authority to control the immense crowd, no police, no military forces.

Someone next to me was saying that people had seen and heard reports of guns being sold in the area, ever since July 1839. Another guy said he'd heard that Pidduck, the ironmonger, was involved but someone else shouted over that that was wrong and it was a Birmingham gun-maker, called Thomson. "Ah've seen 'em baying sold at th' coffee shop, owned by Mr Steele in Hope Street." A Chartist from Nantwich, Cheshire, then stated that they were being sold by Mr Salt, at his 'coffee-house and arms depot', again in Hope Street. "I've seen a large stock of guns, pistols, swords, bayonets and, pike-heads in his shop." Whispers started going round that they had also heard reports, from others, that gunpowder and explosives had been seen in the shop.

I was determined that I would be at the meeting planned for 6 the next morning. John said he would be there too as he couldn't have me being there on my own - there could well be more violence on the streets. He'd have to give some excuse or other – a damaged hand or something. I said I'd bandage his hand. It was a good idea as he wouldn't be able to work with a sprained or cut hand, even though, he'd have to forego any pay for those days he wasn't able to work.

CHAPTER 11

So we were there the next morning, Tuesday, 16th August 1842, at 6am. There was a lot of laughter and high spirits amongst the crowd. I could see that quite a few were still drunk from the night before. Listening to people there is seemed that the violence hadn't ended last night. Cooper had closed his meeting at dusk and a drunken group decided to make their way to the Rev Aitkins' house, who was on the Board of Guardians at Stoke Workhouse, along with Rev Vale. They knew he had wine cellars and they wanted more. Someone called Edward was shouting out, "Thomas Owen – ay's oor man, ay's oor leader – up went 'is orders – 'Way ur the boys, way con do eet' – so way all charged een efter 'im." Rev Aitkins' wine cellars were soon emptied and their contents consumed by the mob, which consisted of men, women and boys. Aitkins was left without even the walls to his house, with the whole building reduced to rubble. Thomas Owen had gone in, as their leader, and knocked the window sashes out and began throwing furniture out onto the fire in front of the house. Everyone else had followed suit. Someone else shouted out that he'd got several plated candlesticks from the house. Someone called Joseph Whiston, who I found out was a potter and

Methodist lay preacher, was claiming, "Eet wuz may oo wuz fost te foir 'is 'ouse. Theer a skinny bonch o' payple. They keer nothink fer thay poor boggers onder theer care. Ah deed eet in the Lard's neeme, the Lard's judgement on 'em."

I heard Charles Meigh's name mentioned so tried to inch closer to the speaker. It seemed that Charles Meigh was lucky. A foreman at his works, Thomas Jones, paid seven sovereigns to Richard Croxton, leading the riot at his works, to move the mob along past the Meigh's pottery, without incident. However, that wasn't enough, "Skinny bustard," was the term used, and that Charles Meigh had, in fact, to send out for an extra three pounds, as the mob felt seven pounds was too little. Richard Croxton added, "Ah ought te 'ev 'ad three toims seven sovereigns, fer ah cud 'ev caused th bloody place te 'ev bin barnt dine."

William Parker, the county magistrate, wasn't so fortunate. They left his property, Albion House, in ruins – just a burnt-out shell, without so much as a roof. They also destroyed the house of Mr Forrester, who was agent to Earl Granville.

By this time, some of the rioters, maybe conscious of the crimes they were committing, or beginning to sober up, had begun to blacken their faces, whilst others attempted to disguise themselves by dressing as women.

The meeting started, but there was no sign of Cooper. I wondered where he was, especially as he'd called the meeting.

William Ellis was there encouraging the crowd to continue until the Charter became the law of the land.

Joseph Capper took the chair. There was such a huge crowd that I couldn't hear him properly. All I managed to hear was "Thousands of striking men from Manchester and Stockport have bivouacked during the night in the streets of Leek. They have got more support along the way. They are to meet us at Burslem. Those who cannot afford to get guns must get pikes, and those who cannot afford to get either, must get torches." At this, a cry went up and a show of arms was raised in the air, revealing a whole range of sticks, pikes, coshes and whatever the crowd had been able to lay their hands on. They looked a motley crew of half-starved, dirty, itinerants, but these sunken cheeked faces were angrily shouting and screaming for vengeance. They'd had a taste of yesterday's warfare and were out for more.

William Ellis, continuing Joseph Capper's furore that he'd aroused in the crowd, urged the crowd on "Now me lads, we have got the parson's house down, we must have the churches down, for if we lose this day, we lose the day forever." And with a loud shout to the crow, at the top of his voice, "So, now lads, for Burslem and now to business." Then a huge roar went up and the crowd was on the move in a massive, orderly procession, led by women. John and I joined the crowd. I was feeling excited in a sort of way but totally out of my depth and scared. I'd never even been on a friendly march before and this was a riot. We had to keep our wits about us, try to keep away from the troubles that, undoubtedly, were going to erupt on entering Burlem. We had no intension of taking part, just watching proceedings.

The crowd was singing:

"The lion of freedom's let loose from his den,
And we'll rally round him again and again."

On a little hill in the vast valley was spread out the Indian-red architecture of Bursley (the local name for Burslem) —tall chimneys and rounded ovens, schools. John pointed out the buildings to me as we walked - the new scarlet market, the grey tower of the old church, the high spire of the Evangelical church, the low spire of the church of genuflexions, and the crimson chapels, and rows of little red houses with amber chimney pots, and the gold angel of the blackened town hall topping the whole. It looked so picturesque - from a distance!

We entered Burslem at about nine that morning in formidable numbers. The market place of Burslem was considered some of the most valuable property in the town but was no less offensive, in fact worse with open soil drains leading from privies in the back yards. The marketplace, was dominated in the centre by the town hall, mainly Georgian in scale and containing many brick and stucco frontages. Near the parish church was a filthy open mud-hole, receiving sewers and filth, presumably for manure.

On the south side several houses stood, among them the impressive Leopard Hotel, having the central doorway flanked by three-storied semi-circular bays. A little further west was the Commercial Bank – a most striking, elegant building having a tall frontage of stone ashlar, built in the Italian style with Venetian windows

At the south-east corner of the marketplace, facing Moorland Road, was the Big House. John advised that it had been built by the brothers Thomas and John Wedgwood in the mid 18th century. It was the most important residence in the town and still is the only house of any quality. A three-storey house, of red brick with stone dressings, and five bays;

the central bay projecting slightly and being surmounted by a pediment. The window lintels are of rusticated stone and the central windows are emphasised by stone architraves; below them is a pedimented port supported on Doric columns, with a walled forecourt and entrance gates.

The Big House, built 1750

http://www.thepotteries.org/walks/burslem/big_house.jpg

We didn't have any time left for looking around. The mob, on entering Chapel Square, had joined up with another mob already there. Looking back to the 'Swan Inn' in Swan Square, which we'd passed, we saw another mob breaking into the 'George Inn' nearby, helping themselves to drink. I saw someone throwing money in the air and people making a grab for it, so, obviously the tills or money drawers had been forced open. Just then a group of soldiers appeared and drove them out. Voices shouted out that it was Major Trench of the 2nd Dragoons. They must have been stationed there overnight to get there so quickly. It looked like he had 50 or so men with him. From what I could make out, the dragoons were only using the flats of their swords, I could see them gleaming in the sun. So, presumably the dragoons were issuing a friendly warning, at this time.

I saw a man striking out at the dragoons, using a large stick – "Thut's Cogsey Nelly" John said beside me. "Ay's one ev the three oo claimbed the Town Hall tower and brok the new clock. Ay woz imprisoned but got broke owt."

"Hooray for Cogsey Nelly!" came the repeated cry from the crowd. Seeing Cogsey Nelly fighting back, the crowd took it upon themselves to start throwing stones and every pane of glass in the building was quickly broken.

Cognsey was soon captured by the dragoons.

This was the second serious injury of the kind which Mr Barlow, the landlord, had sustained within a few days, from what I recalled from newspaper reports - his house having been one of the objects of attack on the morning of the 7th.

It was then that I recognised Capt Powys, on horseback. He looked magnificent on his chestnut steed. He was erect in his saddle, straight backed with sword, raised, glistening in the sunlight. He looked resplendent in his red jacket with yellow facings, white waistcoat, white leather breaches and military boots. His helmet bore a bearskin crest with a feather at the side. He rode to the top of St. John's Square, placed himself in a prominent position, in full sight of the crowd in Market Place and read the Riot Act in the loudest voice he could muster.

"OUR SOVEREIGN LADY, THE QUEEN, CHARGETH AND COMMANDETH ALL PERSONS, BEING ASSEMBLED, IMMEDIATELY TO DISPERSE THEMSELVES, AND PEACEABLY TO DEPART TO THEIR HABITATIONS, OR TO THEIR LAWFUL BUSINESS, UPON THE PAINS CONTAINED

IN THE ACT MADE IN THE FIRST YEAR OF KING GEORGE THE FIRST, FOR PREVENTING TUMULTS AND RIOTOUS ASSEMBLIES. GOD SAVE THE QUEEN."

About 200 Special Constables, under the command of Samuel Alcock - a local pottery manufacturer and chief constable of Burslem, along with a few Metropolitan Police Officers assembled behind the troops ready for action. Samuel Alcock, it seemed, had hastily organised these special constables in advance, from among the friends of law and social order of all classes of society, having been made aware of the oncoming mob.

The police officers looked decidedly worse for wear, as though they'd been helping themselves to free ale, probably in the 'Legs of Man' Inn on the corner of Fountain Place and Market Place. They looked a bit scared, not at all ready for a fray, some trying to hide behind others.

Another troop of 2nd Dragoon Guards from Newcastle appeared, this troop under the command of Major French.

More and more people were gathering, some presumably onlookers, the same as me and John.

Capt. Powys had ridden onto Chapel Bank, just passed where we were standing and again read the Riot Act, asking those, who were quietly disposed, to go home. He rode back past us to the market square and read the Riot Act again.

No-one was moving, not even the on-lookers and roars of protest went up from the crowd, in all directions. They weren't going anywhere. After a couple of minutes of stand-off, it looked like Capt. Powys had made up his mind and his command of "CLEAR THE STREETS" rang out through the air. On that order a tumultuous rattle of swords being drawn from their scabbards echoed around the square and the cry went up, "CHARGE". The soldiers then drove in upon the mob, but again only used the flat side of the swords. The crowd were screaming and running in all directions but such were the narrow streets or Shambles of the market place that they disappeared down streets and reappeared up others. Burslem market place had many outlets, and these enabled the people to baffle somewhat the attacks of the soldiers. This small success of the crowd had fired them with greater daring, and they reappeared in the market place, attacking the soldiers and police en masse with sticks and stones, not giving a hoot as to their own safety. Some, who had become separated in the roads, were attacked and maimed; in my mind like a lion running after a herd of gazelle and pouncing on the weakest that could not keep up or had fallen.

This attack lasted for about an hour with the dragoons and special police trying to marshal the crowd.

I was holding onto John in all this mayhem, taking shelter behind the fairly low walls of the Big House.

Just then there came piercing sounds from a huge band of people, marching along Moorland Road, behind us, and a crowd singing to the accompanying band, "See the Conquering Hero Comes". A cry went up, "They're coming from Leek" and a wild shout of "Hooray". There must have been anything from 6000 to 8000 men, armed with cudgels, or furnished with stones. Then they were shouting, yelling like madmen and waving weapons, which could be seen by those at the top of the market place. On hearing this, the soldiers left the market place galloped towards us at the Big House. The hooves were like thunder, the ground shook.

I cowered beneath John's arm, behind the wall. The shouting was raucous and I covered my ears to try to block it out. I couldn't stop shaking and I felt that my knees could not support me any longer. This was the end, one of those swords was going to prod down over the wall and rip right through me. "Oh God, give me strength", I muttered to myself in a silent prayer.

The galloping stopped. The dragoons had halted in front of the new mob, just past the Big House at the top of Moorland Road. I gained enough courage to peek out at them, though still crouched down. They'd come from Leek, Congleton and Macclesfield, from the banners they held aloft, weavers most of them, although I noticed that there were no be-starred Chartist flags as I'd seen yesterday, which seemed odd to me. Obviously these rioters hadn't been incited by the Chartists. They were a whole different kettle of fish, but I could see that the Chartists demonstrations would be linked to these rioters anyway. They looked poor wretches, mostly half-dressed and half-starved – pale- faced and cadaverous looking. They didn't look like a formidable force. The only really vigorous men looked like agricultural labourers, not part of the original crew, who had probably joined them on their march. Many of them carried thick sticks in their thin arms.

Most were using their torn aprons and handkerchiefs to hold things, presumably stones they'd picked up along the way, which they now commenced throwing at the troops, advancing all the time.

The lily-livered Special Constables had now gathered – I couldn't tell which group looked the more white-faced, they or the crowd. I gathered from John that these would be ordinary working men, taken on just today. They wouldn't be trained and would be friends and neighbours, or even relatives, of the people they were being asked to fight against.

"What do you want?" came the trumpeting voice of Capt. Powys.

The reply came quick, "Our rights and liberties, the Charter and more to eat."

This was taken up by the whole crowd, "MORE TO EAT", shouted out repeatedly. "MORE TO EAT, MORE TO EAT, MORE TO EAT", together with thumping of sticks and feet on the ground, in rhythm.

Capt. Powys voice resonated above the crowd, "Assembling in a disorderly mob is not the way to your rights and liberties. I entreat you to disperse and go quietly to your homes."

This advice was received with mocking and defiant yells, such "We will not be moved", "Get off your rocking horse, little boy, and go home yourself." "You're entreating no-one – go and entreat yourself." (or words to that effect).

I mean, what were they meant to do? Capt. Powys did not tell these men how to get their rights and liberties. They had tried to get them by more orderly agitation for 12 years and failed. Parliament wasn't listening to them. He was telling them to go quietly to their own homes but these homes were places robbed of nearly all the elements which make a home. They were places where they saw the pinched faces of wives and children, and heard cries for food, which they could not supply. To reason in this way with these men was quite "proper" for a military magistrate, but it can be seen that to take such advice would have been a miracle of self-restraint, and such miracles are not wrought by the grace of starvation.

Someone in the crowd started shouting out a Chartist song, taken up by the rest:

"Rude comparisons you draw,
Words refuse to sate your maw,
Your gaunt limbs the cobweb law
Cannot hold.

You're not clogged with foolish pride,
But can seize a right denied,
Somehow God is on your side,
Hunger and cold."

The yell of defiance which rose from the crowd in response to Capt. Powy's words was wholly of the devil's inspiration. Violence had been done to the rights and liberties of these men as wicked as the violence which was now provoked.

The quote came into my head: "To destroy life and property is as stupid as it is iniquitous, but let us recognise that it is equally stupid and iniquitous to provoke a destroying desperation." or something like that. I don't remember who said it, oh yes, must have been Charles Shaw, the book the teacher at the nursing home told me to read.

The yell of defiance was a signal for action. There went forth the cry, "We'll make the soldiers run and duck the specials behind." Showers of stones were hurled at the soldiers and the mob pressed forward with those in front touching the horses' heads. That seething mass of desperation had been released and must be resisted by the troops.

Capt. Powys had shown remarkable restraint up to this ominous moment but collision was now inevitable and there went forth from his lips the fatal ringing cry to his soldiers.

"FIRE".

Immediately the guns were raised and a rattle of musketry started. The crowd shrank back instinctively, but vainly, owing to its own mass. The musketry rattled, but the rattle was soon drowned by cries of defiance and terror and agony from that writhing mass of human beings. Numbers fell to the ground, either wounded or forced down by the trampling of horses on human flesh, which followed the firing of the muskets.

Maddened but still desperate, the crowd broke and fled in different directions. Many were knocked over and trampled by the fleeing masses, others were injured by the blows from the troops and specials that were now in hot pursuit. I saw a man go down, shot in the back. Standing just in front of the walls of the Big House was a young man with a stone in one hand and a stick in the other. He had just thrown a large stone at the troops at the same moment as the order to fire was given. One soldier saw him, aimed and fired. His brains were blown out against the gate-post. The sound of the rifle reverberated against the wall of the Big House and I saw splatters of blood rising into the air above me. I felt my mouth opening to emit a scream but the next I knew was that John was holding his hand over my mouth and my head against his chest, to stifle my screams and prevent me from running and being seen ….. I was crying violently, sobbing but somehow silently with my whole body convulsing. I don't know how I kept those sobs down to low moans. Was I to be found by the guards and shot on sight or suffocated against John's chest. I had to breathe so I found myself edging up John's chest and nestling into his neck. John was rubbing my back softly, in a calming action, but still holding me tight, whilst whispering soft, 'shh, shh' sounds gently in my ear. (**Note 5**)

https://en.wikipedia.org/wiki/File:Potteries_Riot_1842_.jpg,

This was the first real opposition the crowd had faced since the start of the riots and they started screaming in panic, fleeing in every direction, trying to get away. They were terrified by this onslaught. So many shots were fired and, although many were not killed outright, nevertheless, many were wounded and were carried away by friends, or hobbled away themselves. People were being knocked over and trampled by the fleeing masses; others were injured by blows from the troops and specials that were now in hot pursuit. I imagine some died slow and lingering deaths from infected wounds as they couldn't report to a surgeon, otherwise it would be known that they were at the riot and would be arrested and possibly even suffer the fate of deportation.

The crowd had left the immediate area with the troops and police after them. When John felt it was safe to stand up, we started walking, past the dead body of the young boy at the gate. I was still holding onto John to stop myself falling. I didn't know what direction we were going in, I was shell-shocked and confused.

John was mumbling something to himself and was holding onto a locket on a chain around his neck.

"What's that" I asked weakly.

"Aw, ah 'olds onte eet when ah'm fayling a mite worrit. Ah says a little prayer en th 'ope shay's looking dine on may en con protect may."

"Is it a religious symbol or a cross?"

"Nay, ducky, eet's a ring. Me wife's wedding ring. Ah put eet on a chain rund may neck so shay'll allays bay wi' may."

"I didn't know you'd been married, John, what happened to her?"

"She dayed, ef th' cholera, abite fayve years ago, 1st October 1837 te bay presays. Ah nearly dayed wi' har, but dinna in th'end. Shay woz the lov o' may laif, may Alice. Ah still miss har."

"Oh, how sad for you, John."

"Oor naymes 'r on eet. Ah gor eet engraved, says – Alice and John."

"How beautiful, John" I replied, while looking at the ring, "She'll keep you safe, don't worry. I'm sure she's looking after you."

We carried on walking. Streams of people passed us, some limping through small wounds they had received, or perhaps from the terrible crush in which they had been carried along. We saw another man shot. He wasn't quite dead - the bullet having entered his back and passed out through his throat. Friends were trying to get him out of the way and get help for him. Most were rushing down the Leek New Road as if they were pursued by wild beasts. Some of these had portions of their clothes torn off and were only half dressed. Just outside the town we came upon a man and a woman, who were excitedly relating the perils and sufferings they had just been through. The man was a little cobbler. John knew him from Tunstall. This poor, little cobbler wore a tall hat, and the crown of it was cut clean off. The bridge of his nose, too, was neatly slit in two. The blood was trickling to the end of it and forming red drops there. He obviously didn't have a handkerchief with him as he kept wiping off the red drops with the back of his hand, so his hand was covered in blood, as a butcher's, cutting up meat. When we approached him he was telling a group of people how a horse soldier had made at him with a bloody purpose and cut off the crown of his hat with the first blow. "'E was intending to cut me yed off as 'e made another slash at me with 'is sword, but ah ducked and saved me yed. Ah was trying to get away but 'e follahed me and slashed out again with 'is sword. Ah was lucky, ah just threw me yed back just in time and the point of the sword only went through the bridge of me nose. Ah managed to escape 'im at last by mingling with the crowd. 'E was a ferocious bugger, out for the kill! Ah'm fair shaking." He carried on in that vein, swearing and cussing the solder, calling him all the names under the sun.

Near to the cobbler stood a woman, who had been wounded in the leg. This wound had evidently been the result of a spent bullet, as she was moving away from the crowd. Her dress was badly torn and she looked as if she had been rolled down the shord-ruck (*Rubbish tip containing waste moulds, saggars and faulty ware such as lump or wasters. A heap of broken crockery!*), on the Leek New Road from Burslem. She, too, had her story to tell, but it was interrupted with so many hysterical outbursts and digressions that it would have puzzled me, as a shorthand writer, to have given a clear and connected account of it.

The sight which presented itself was confusing and bewildering in the extreme. It was evident that masses of people had remained stolidly defiant or curious, even after the fatal charge by the soldiers had been made. There were hundreds of people packed in the narrow streets at the back of the shambles, right down to the Big House, where the boy had been shot.

The market place presented a weird and dismal aspect. All the shops were closed, and the soldiers were busy driving the slowly-moving and sullen-faced crowds away. Windows were broken in the Town Hall, and many other signs of destructive work were to be seen.

The more furious part of the mob had been driven out of the market-place, but streams of people were pouring into it again from the many side places of access. There were evidently gathering elements for another outbreak, and at last the word was given to the military to clear the market-place.

The soldiers were driving the people along, whilst the special constables were placed opposite every avenue to the market-place to prevent a fresh rush of people. The soldiers' horses were prancing, some rearing up and braying, and the soldiers' swords gleamed as they pressed upon every section of the mob.

We had managed to get ourselves to the back of the Shambles by this time, but kept well up above the mass of the people, so that we could see what was going on without being entangled in the crowd. The horse solders came up this narrow street, pressing loosely on the heels of the people, and using the flat sides of their swords upon those they could reach.

Owing to the dense pressure of the crowd, running was impossible, and numbers of people had fallen over themselves, landing in heaps of flailing arms and legs, through the pressure or terror. The confusion and groans and shrieks were terrible to hear and see, for men, women and even children, made up this seething mass.

We were standing above the crowd and looking down on bareheaded men and women, with their hair streaming about their faces. Their hats, caps, bonnets and shawls had been wrestled off in the scramble, and lay on the ground, to be trodden into the mud by the thousands of feet and horse hooves. Without their hair coverings, we could clearly see the agony and fear depicted on their faces. It was a sight of terror never to be forgotten. It seemed a cruel thing, too, to drive those who were not there to fight, and to hurry and frighten them in this manner.

We made our way back to the New Road we saw special constables forming a cordon on the left-hand side of the market-place to keep the crowd moving on and stop them disappearing into side streets.

When we all came out into the wider area up near Greenhead, the crowd broke away as fast as their legs could carry them until they got into the New Road and the road leading to High Lane. There they stopped and turning, weeping fitfully and screaming, began to spout out back towards the troops and special constables all the insults and grievances a person could muster against the crushing injustices that had been done to them and cursing the land in which they had been born. They only wanted to work and to live a reasonable life by their labour.

CHAPTER 12

We were making our way back to Ash Hall. There were still crowds milling about but causing no trouble.

A great tiredness came over me, probably the adrenaline had died down as I started to relax. I realised that neither of us had had anything to eat or drink all day. I left without breakfast as we had to get to Hanley so early in the morning. It had been a long walk to Burslem and would be a long walk back. I had to get a drink or something to eat as I just had no energy, but all the shops were still boarded up.

John suggested going back through the fields, as it might be a more direct route and to steer away from the crowds milling around the streets. The fields would be dry as it was summer. Anything to get back more quickly, so I agreed. We made our way back to Moorland Road, where the young boy had been killed right in front of us. The body, fortunately, had been taken away but the splattered blood was still there spread over the road and wall of the Big House. We crossed the New Road heading for Sneyd Green, going through the forest towards Birches Head. At Abbey Farm, John jumped over a wall into a field. He'd seen some carrots growing and dug some out. There weren't many left as I suppose they had been raided by starving people. He washed the earth off in the River Trent, which ran through the farm. There were also bushes along the way with ripening raspberries, blackberries and blueberries. I also found a couple of wild strawberries growing under the bushes. They were so refreshing and bucked me up a little. Then we got back onto the road and followed it, crossing the Leek Road and finding Greasley Road, leading onto Eaves Lanes. Just past Eaves Farm I felt that I really couldn't go any further. My knees were buckling under me, and I told John I had to rest.

"Thar's a little strame just through the ferm, a futpath laydes te eet. Con yer git yarsel thar. The wayter will refresh yer, Jane. Eet's gud wayter, no laik the Trent."

So, I gathered up what little strength I had and trudged after him. He was right. The water was so cool. I drank from it and splashed it over my face, neck, arms and legs.

While walking, I took it upon myself to broach the subject of John's wife. He was a bit hesitant at first but I found out they'd been married for four years. They got married on 1 June 1833. It was a great day, lovely and sunny, and all the workmen and friends attended the church, with a spread and drinks afterwards to celebrate. John had been working at Mr Meigh's pottery in Hanley and they rented a little worker's cottage from him. He and his wife, Alice, had been really happy and they were finally expecting their first child, but then the worst thing happened. Cholera was rife in the town and his wife succumbed to it. John hadn't mentioned about the baby earlier. Maybe that was just one step too much for him in the life-threatening scenario back in Burslem. But now I saw a tear come to John's light blue eyes and he began to weep softly, wiping the tears away with the back of his hand. It was a poignant moment. Tears seemed so strange on this beefy, resolute man, who looked like he would fend off the devil himself to save his own, but it's always the biggest who fall the hardest, so the saying goes. John said that he'd tried what he could to nurse her through it, but he couldn't help her and she finally died of the cholera, along with his unborn child. He continued to say that he'd gone into such a state of depression afterwards that he could not settle to work again at the pottery and the little cottage held nothing but sadness for him, full of memories, so he found himself just wandering, sleeping outside wherever he finally found himself, too exhausted to continue. His money had dwindled and he found himself begging for food. His brother tried to help but they had a house full of children and no money to spare. Everyone has their breaking point and John had found his. I felt really sad for him and gave him a hug.

As it happened, Mr Meigh had been worried about him and sent out scouts to try to find him. He'd had a good opinion of John and his work and didn't want to lose a good man. Finally finding him, Mr Meigh saw that he was in no fit state to carry on at the pottery. He, instead, suggested an outside job, in the fresh air, might help build up his spirits. Mr Meigh gave him the opportunity of working for him to build Ash Hall, helping build the house and lay out the gardens. Mr Meigh had bought the ground and old hall in 1837 and was in the process of building a new hall. John added that Mr Meigh was a good man to his workers, one of the few - if he felt the worker was worth the while.

I'd not noticed the rain clouds gathering. It looked like we were going to have one of those sudden summer storms.

The wind was swirling up, sweeping around the trees and bushes and blowing dust along the path. It had got decidedly chillier all of a sudden as well, and must be quite late. Yes, the sun was beginning to set behind us, over Hanley. So, I'd been up and about since five this morning and now it was about nine in the evening – a long, perilous, terrifying day. I wanted to be tucked up in my bed, following a hot drink and something to eat. The rain really started to splatter down now, with thunder and flashes of lightning. There was nowhere to shelter so we just had to carry on. I put my shawl over my head and John took off his jacket to act as an umbrella over both of us. We arrived at Eaves Lane and followed the footpaths skirting Wetley Moor, passing Long Field, Slack Pit Field, and Green Field, which led to the Bridle Path, just by Ash House. John said that these fields contained old coal mine shafts and you had to be very careful crossing them and best stick to the paths.

Just as we were approaching Bridle Path we heard a roaring commotion of a number of raised voices. The ruckus was coming from Ash Hall. "Sounds like there's more trouble, John."

"Indayed, God 'elp us." And he started to run down Bridle Path and out to the entrance of Ash Hall. There was no other way through. I followed as quickly as my legs could carry me but I couldn't keep up, I was just too tired. 'Come on, adrenaline,' I said to myself. Get moving, though what I was meant to do when I got there, God only knows.

What greeted me on entering the driveway to Ash House was another mob, who were obviously still livid following their treatment in Burslem. They still had fire in their hearts and the rain hadn't dampened their spirits.

It looked like Job Meigh had been warned of their approach as they'd marched up Ash Bank. He was standing on the steps in front of the Hall. The door was half open and from my viewpoint I could see, through the window as the curtains had been left open, Joseph Weston, the coachman, placing hats, cloaks and coats on chairs and wherever in that front room – one coat after another – I didn't know where they were all coming from. Maybe Mr Meigh had guests and he'd asked for the coats to be hung on backs of chairs to dry after the downpour. I couldn't work it out.

Mr Meigh was having an argument with people in the crowd. They were stating their demands and Mr Meigh was refuting them, giving examples of his own generosity towards his workforce.

Theirs were the demands that we had heard earlier in Burslem, more money, food, a decent living and so on. "I state to you beseechingly that the people who worked for me have found me to be a man who has looked after his workers. Yes, I have a luxurious lifestyle in comparison to your own, as have most other pottery owners, but not at the expense of my workers. I am not one of those. I have looked after my workers. I have provided sickness benefits for them. I have made sure they had dwellings. I have made sure they had regular work so they could earn enough to feed their families."

"Yer still filthy reech, en cayre nowt fer the loiks ef us." and similar cries were being shouted out as Mr Meigh tried to state his case.

Claim and counter-claim, challenge and rebuttal, allegation and refutation flowed to and fro in a noisy torrent. It looked as though, whatever he said, Mr Meigh was not going to win the argument. They were out for blood and I didn't know what was holding them back. I'd heard talk of a secret tunnel leading under the Hall to Ash House over the main road. I didn't know if it existed but I couldn't see Mr Meigh getting out of this one – but then again, I couldn't see him running and letting his lovely new Hall get burnt to the ground, as they had done with so many other buildings.

The rain had stopped. I saw John at the back of the crowd and went to stand by him. John put his arm around me to fend off the mass of bodies. I looked up to Mr Meigh and saw a look of recognition come into his eyes. This was followed immediately by a sneer that crept across his face. Was that because he'd seen John with his arm around me? Surely not? Then he turned towards the crowd again.

He continued, "I've even taken it upon myself to look into the toxins present in the paintwork used on my pots. I have carried out copious research into this, all to prevent my workforce from suffering needlessly from poisons contained in them. I don't know if you've seen in the grounds but there are small pools along the stream, and a water wheel. There I have mixed the colours and tested them. These trials have been tested and manufacturers only use these new glazes now. This has been my work, to aid all pottery workers, to prevent them from having to ingest poisonous substances, either through the skin, or breathing in toxins."

Mr Meigh was trying to edge the crowd further around towards the windows of the front-facing room.

Just then someone shouted out. He'd seen the outdoor raiments apparently drying in that front room., "Hay lads, owd up, hay's got a bliddy army in theer. Ay's trying te trick us." The mob paused, its resolution broke, its solidarity crumbled and away it began to drift, slowly and then with increasing rapidity, as rain drops, once more, began to blow over Ash Bank.

John and I stayed stock still where we were with Job Meigh's eyes burning into us. A hard, black stare, even though I knew he had blue eyes.

John was the first to break the silence. "Way saw 'em en kem running te 'elp yer, Mr Meigh, sir."

"HELP ME", Job Meigh screamed. "It was YOU who brought them here!

"No sir, way kem fer ov'r t' moors."

"You've both been out with these rioters all day. I have my spies too, don't you know. You've been seen."

I added, "We just wanted to come back and report to you, sir. We've not been involved in any of the atrocities."

"You shouldn't have been there in the first place. You've left my wife on her own, to fend for herself, with no offer of assistance so she could not leave her room. You should both be ashamed of yourselves. Call yourself a carer – you haven't cared a fig for her."

"I'm sorry, sir, it was something I had to do and regret doing it now."

"Sorry, doesn't begin to spread oil on the stormy waters that you have created. And what do you mean 'it was something I had to do'," he said imitating a young belligerent girl's voice. "What you had to do was be here. Instead you bring a marauding crowd direct to my door, ready to burn the house down and me with it."

He went inside for a second and came out with a load of leaflets and papers that we'd picked up on our visits to the Chartist meetings. He threw them at us. "So, you're nothing to do with these rioters and so-called Chartists? I found them in your room, girl, and that villain's work room (pointing to John). So, what are all these - letters back home? I've had enough of your excuses.

And you, Mr Wood, after all I did for when your work suffered at the factory after the death of your wife. Do I warrant this disservice? You and your lover are just dead meat now." At my quizzical look to 'lover' he resumed. "Don't think I didn't notice his arm around you. How long has this been going on? I should whip you from here to kingdom come!" and he strode towards the stables.

"Run, John, run for your life. I'll be right behind you."

John ran towards the Wetley Moors and fields to the north of the Hall and I was running for my life behind him. I had no time to think where I was going, just trying not to stumble on the tufts of uneven grass. It was dark now, just the light from a semi moon, so could hardly see a thing. My ears were just so sensitively pitched to hear the slightest sound from behind. We came across a hedge, too high to jump, but managed find a place to crawl through, then both of us continued running. I was panting heavily, out of breathe. John was now some way up in front. He was running through a copse of trees up ahead.

Then behind me I heard the heavy galloping of a horse's hooves. I took a sneak look behind me and there was Job Meigh charging towards us on horseback. So, he'd gone to swiftly saddle his horse and collect his whip, which he was lashing in the air. I scrambled to the trees, hoping this would give some cover and slow down the horse. I scrambled through a stream and exited the copse on the other side.

There I saw the vague silhouette of John running over Long Field.

Just then, Job Meigh appeared. The horse had jumped the fence and Job Meigh had continued on the path around the copse, jumping the stream. I should have stayed in the wood, but my mind was too much of a mess and, instead, continued after John. Job Meigh was soon over me and whipped me to the ground, knocking the last bit of breathe out of me. I couldn't move, as Job Meigh advanced his horse towards the running John.

He was trying to dodge the horse, running to the left of it then zigzagging, but it was no use. I saw John turn round and raise his arms over his face as the horse was nearing his shoulder. The horse reared on its hind legs as Job Meigh's whip came down across John's body and he stumbled to his knees, but was up again and running. I got up and stumbled after them. Job Meigh's whip hit home again and I heard a scream, then couldn't see John any more. Job Meigh turned his horse around and came after me again but, at the last second, turned the horse towards home. He shouted, "Never darken my doors again, you whoring slut!"

I scrambled to where I last saw John. It was a gaping, black hole that had been somewhat overgrown, hiding the entrance to one of the old coal shafts that John had warned me about.

I called out over and over, "John, John, can you hear me. Are you OK." But no answer came. I was sobbing violently, tears bubbling up, down on my knees, peering down the hole, rocking backwards and forwards with grief. I was in pain from the whiplash but that didn't outweigh the pain I was feeling for the loss of John.

When I finally stopped crying, which seemed like an eternity, I looked round just to make sure Job Meigh wasn't hovering, then turned back again. That's when I realised that I was back in my nurse's uniform and coat and my bag was beside me. The drag long skirt, shawl, apron and bonnet had gone…..

I staggered shakily to my feet. I still felt like I'd been whipped. I felt for a weal from the lashing, but could not discern one. I still had the feeling that I wanted to give one last call out for John, but I knew that would be a fond idea – he would be dead about 170 years now.

I made my way, slowly and painfully back to the nursing home. I had no idea of the reception I would receive. Had the police been involved in my disappearance?

I stumbled up the steps and Molly greeted me with a, "Hello again, have you forgotten something?"

I don't remember anything after that, I must have fainted.

CHAPTER 13

I woke up in what looked like a hospital bed. Molly had obviously raised the alarm when I'd collapsed.

There was a buzzer by the bed, which I used and one of the doctors soon appeared.

"Well, now, Jane. Glad to see you're in the land of the living. Care you tell us what you remember after leaving the nursing home, yesterday, after your shift?"

Yesterday, so, all the months I'd been away, haven't counted in the here and now. No-one had missed me and, presumably, I still had a job.

As I hadn't answered, the doctor continued, "Looks like you're still a bit groggy, Jane. Here, have a drink of water. I've taken your blood pressure and a blood sample and we haven't found anything out of the ordinary. Do you remember anything after leaving the nursing home, after your shift, yesterday?" I still didn't answer as I didn't know what to say. What could I say – that I'd been transported back in time and undergone an horrific episode, seen a good friend die right in front of me, and not been able to do anything about it. No-one would believe me.

I sipped the water and thought. Maybe I had made it

all up. Maybe I'd had some sort of psychotic episode – but it was all so real.

"I was mugged", I finally blurted out. "I fought him off but it was dark so I couldn't see his face properly. Anyway, I don't think he got away with anything but my back still hurts."

"Ok, let's have a look at your back." I sat up and the doctor examined my back. He prodded me in various places and I let out little moans of pain. "Yes, obviously you have some tenderness there but I can't see any bruising" the doctor replied. "You could have possibly been hit over the back with some weapon or other. If this is the case, we need to contact the police."

My mind was a haze of muddled thoughts. I still couldn't work out whether I'd dreamt the whole episode, although the doctor had said there was some tenderness in my back but then again, there was no bruising. Could this by psychosomatic, I thought to myself? Could my 'dream' have caused me to feel real pain? If the police were informed, what should I tell them, that I'd had a dream, that I'd dreamt the incident of John falling down the mine shaft? Do I ask them to look for bones of a possible murder from over 170 years ago? Had my mind gone into overdrive while sleeping, after listening to Mr Shelton's history of the period and reading Charles Shaw's book?

My mind was still a blur when lunch was delivered. I was starving. The nurse said the police had been called and were waiting to interview me. She advised that there was a private room we could go to off the ward if I wished.

After I had eaten, a detective was shown in, DI Barratt. I threw a dressing gown on and we went to the private room.

"I understand you have been the victim of a mugging." DI Barratt commenced.

"That's not exactly right," I interrupted.

"OK, tell me in your own words, Miss Paget, what actually happened?"

"I really don't know how to start, or in fact how much you'll believe or indeed how much is real."

"Sorry, Miss Paget, what do you mean, how much is real. Have you got me here under false pretences? You do know this will not be looked on kindly if you are wasting police time?"

"Oh, no, I don't want to waste police time but I'm still confused. Everything seems like a dream to me. I don't know what is real and what isn't."

"OK, let's start at the beginning. What's the last thing you remember, whether you feel it's a false memory, a dream or whatever? Just take your time. You obviously were found on the steps of Ash Hall Nursing Home, where I believe you are employed, yesterday evening, and were brought here. What led up to your being there, at that time, in such a state of exhaustion and distress that you collapsed?"

"OK", I stuttered, "whether you believe me or not, here goes. I was running after a good friend, John Woods. We had got to a field over the back of the nursing home. We were being chased, on horseback, by Job Meigh, the previous owner of Ash Hall. He had a whip in his hand which he used on me as he rode past to get to John. It was dark. John tried all he could to sidestep, get out of the way of the whip coming down on him, but Job Meigh just carried on whipping him. The next I knew John had disappeared. He'd fallen….. down one of the old mine pits. Job Meigh then rode off. I called and called, but there was no answer. John's still there in the pit."

"OK, miss, thank you." DI Barratt immediately got on his phone to contact the station, asking for the fire brigade and ambulance to be brought to the field at the back of the nursing home. He also asked for an investigation on Job Meigh, anything that was known about him, previous record, where he lived, mental history and so on.

"I could show you exactly where the pit is, if you wish. I understand there are a few pits in that field and it would save time. I'll just throw some clothes on and come with you."

"That would be helpful, miss. As you heard, we'll also be investigating this Job Meigh. Is there anything you could tell me about him? What led up to this incident?"

"I'll tell you everything after we find John, please." I couldn't possibly go into the ins and outs of what would possibly end up being a figment of my imagination. I mean, what if there was no body in the pit. Then again, what if there were? If there were no body, I'd obviously dreamt it all and I could possibly have to undergo a mental health assessment to establish the state of my mind. However, if there were a body, how could I explain how I knew there was a body there – a dream, a psychic experience, being sent back in time to discover the truth of the ghost of Ash Hall? Yes, of course, the figure I had seen from the landing on the first floor of the nursing home was the ghost of John running away from Job Meigh, to his death!

So, I dressed and DI Barratt drove me to the nursing home. An ambulance and the fire brigade were already there. I led the way, back onto the main road, then through Bridle Passage, past the copse of trees and into the Long

Field. There was no way they could get the ambulance and fire engine onto the field from this direction as the path was just that, a narrow earth path between hedges. So, the ambulance and fire engine would be driven back to the main road, right, then right again into Brookhouse Lane, the nearest road to the left of Ash Hall, and would lead onto the field via Hanley Hayes Farm to the north of the field.

I was feeling very unsettled naturally. The last time, in my mind, I was there was last night, being chased by Job Meigh on horseback and the feeling of that whip crashing down on me. I had to stifle a scream. I kept looking back over my shoulder, frightened that Job Meigh would reappear to exact vengeance on me yet again. DI Barratt took me by the arm, and tried to reassure me - he could see how scared I was.

We reached the pit. I wanted to call out, "John" again but stopped myself. My mind was in a whirl drifting from 1842 to the present day and mixing up the two.

A ladder was put down the pit and a fireman descended. His head appeared soon after and he requested a camera. He re-ascended to show the photos to DI Barrett, who came over to me.

"There's no body down there, not one from yesterday anyway. What we have found is a skeleton. So, looks like your John Woods, if he existed, managed to get himself out of the pit."

I tried to interrupt but DI Barrett continued. "As there has been a body at one time, we'll have to get an archaeological team here to investigate further. We can't move the bones ourselves – not our job."

"That IS John Woods," I blurted out.

"Come now, miss. Unless your John Woods was cremated or put in an acid bath overnight, that's not him. You've had a shock of some kind I can see but, be realistic, a pile of bones doesn't appear overnight from a running, living human being the night before. We'd best take you back to the hospital where the doctors can assess you."

"No, I'm not going back there. It is John, I tell you...... and I can prove it."

"OK, I'm listening."

"I don't know if I'm a psychic, I've had no previous experience of seeing figures from the past and, most probably, you coppers poo hoo the idea of psychics, but whether I had a vision or I was transported back in time, I don't know, but I knew John in the year 1842. I think I was shown these visions to find John's body and to give him a proper burial."

"Now, miss, that's all very interesting but I think we should take you back to the hospital."

"No, as I said, I can prove it send the fireman down again. Tell him to look for a necklace with a ring attached to it. He can photograph it first but bring it up. It will have an inscription on it 'Alice and John'." I racked my brain for what John had said in Burslem. "Yes, John and Alice married on 1st June 1833. Alice died of the cholera on 1st October 1837. There should be some way of checking the marriage and death records for those dates, either the council offices or the church records. I beg you, please. Either prove me right and I'm free to go my own way, or prove me wrong and I'll submit to a mental health assessment."

"Well, there's nothing really I can hold you on at the moment, except making up stories and wasting police time. You'll have to come down to the station and submit a written report, pending further investigation into the dates given and possible further mental examination."

I agreed and went back to work for the time being. Everyone was curious about what I'd experienced but, until I was able to prove that the skeleton was that of John, I was saying no more, just that I'd been attacked.

About a week later I had a visit from D I Barratt. He had news.

"We've been through church records for the time and, strangely enough, I have to report that a Miss Alice Simmons and a Mr John Woods were married at Bethseda Church on 1st June 1833. We also found an entry of Alice's death for 1st October 1837."

I gasped a sigh of relief. "So, it's all true. It did happen, I was there in 1842!"

"Well, I don't know if you were there or whether you had a psychic vision but facts are facts. And us 'coppers' don't necessarily 'poo hoo' psychics, in fact we have psychics working with the force on certain unsolved cases. So there, you are free to carry on life as normal as possible and we thank you for your assistance with a very cold case."

"There's just one thing, D I Barratt. Can John's remains now be released from a proper church burial."

"Yes, there's no graveyard at Bethseda Church but there are cemeteries in the neighbourhood. We will provide the necessary release certificate then it's up to you. Presumably there are no descendants of John and Alice as they had no children."

"Ah, but he had a brother, living in Tunstall and they had quite a few children. Could you possibly put me onto someone who might be able to help me find any descendants? You never know, they might be interested."

So, with the help of a contact DI Barratt gave me, we found a number of James' descendants, some still living in the area. A funeral and burial was arranged in Carmountside Cemetery and Crematorium, with some of those descendants attending. I told my story, to astonished faces and John's remains were finally put to rest, never again to haunt Ash Hall Nursing Home.

ALTERNATIVE ENDING

CHAPTER 12

I woke up in what looked like a hospital bed. Molly had obviously raised the alarm when I'd collapsed.

There was a buzzer by the bed, which I used and one of the doctors soon appeared.

"Well, now, Jane. Glad to see you're in the land of the living. Care you tell us what you remember after leaving the nursing home, after your shift, yesterday?"

Yesterday so, all the months I'd been away, haven't counted in the here and now. No-one had missed me and, presumably, I still had a job.

As I hadn't answered, the doctor continued, "Looks like you're still a bit groggy, Jane. Here, have a drink of water. I've taken your blood pressure and a blood sample and we haven't found anything out of the ordinary. Do you remember anything after leaving the nursing home?" I still didn't answer as I didn't know what to say. What could I say – that I'd been transported back in time and undergone an horrific episode, seen a good friend die right in front of me and not been able to do anything about it. No-one would believe me.

I sipped the water and thought. Maybe I had made it

all up. Maybe I'd had some sort of psychotic episode – but it was all so real.

"I was mugged", I finally blurted out. "I fought him off but it was dark so I couldn't see his face properly. Anyway, I don't think he got away with anything but my back still hurts.

"Ok, let's have a look at your back." I sat up and the doctor examined my back. He prodded me in various places and I let out little moans of pain. "Yes, obviously you have some tenderness there but I can't see any bruising" the doctor replied. "You could have possibly been hit over the back with some weapon or other. If this is the case, we need to contact the police."

My mind was a haze of muddled thoughts. I still couldn't work out whether I'd dreamt the whole episode, although the doctor had said there was some tenderness in my back but then again, there was no bruising. Could this by psychosomatic, I thought to myself? Could my 'dream' have caused me to feel real pain? If the police were informed, what should I tell them, that I'd had a dream, that I'd dreamt the incident of John falling down the mine shaft? Do I ask them to look for bones of a possible murder from over 170 years ago? Had my mind gone into overdrive, while sleeping, after listening to Mr Shelton's history of the period and reading Charles Shaw's book?

My mind was still a blur when lunch was delivered. The nurse said the police had been called and were waiting to interview me. She advised that there was a private room we could go to off the ward if I wished.

I was starving and tried to eat, but I was still too upset and pushed the food around on the plate. I then began sobbing into the meal. "**It was all my fault**" I found myself shouting aloud to myself. "I got John to go to Burslem with me. It was me who he came back with. It was me John had his arm round, which had put Job Meigh into such a jealous rage. It was me Job Meigh's spies had seen, in Burslem, with John, mingled up with the mob, trying to escape from the soldiers and police. I led him to his death. **I got him killed. I've got to put this right. I've got to get back. I've got to stop him. I've got to get back. I've got to get back.**"

At that moment a nurse entered the ward. "Hey, what's all this shouting about? Calm down now." I didn't know I was shouting out loud, or indeed what I was saying. In my mind, I wasn't even in the hospital ward, I was back at Ash House listening to the mob shouting abuse at Job Meigh. If I hadn't been there, John would never have been killed. He would have had no reason to go to Burslem, to follow the outraged mob. When the mob finally reached Ash Hall, John would have been there by Job Meigh's side to face the mob together. I had to put this right.

I heard someone saying, from what seemed a long way away, "I'm just going to give you something to help you sleep." and I felt a sharp pain in my arm. I flinched away.

I had a picture in my head of John running along the Bridle Path, in the twilight, to help Job Meigh against the mob. Running, someone running - seeing someone running away from Ash Hall in the twilight. It was the same figure, the same build. It was John who I'd seen from the first floor window at the nursing home, running away. I remembered no more.

I woke up some hours later. It was almost dusk. I was still in a daze, everything was blurry. I remember thinking to myself that I wasn't meant to be there. I had to get back to Ash Hall. I tried to get out of the bed, but was so weak. Something in the back of my mind told me that a nurse had said she was going to give me something to help me sleep. The room seemed to be spinning round and I felt sick. I searched for my clothes and bag and found them hanging up in a wardrobe. I slowly got dressed and made my way out of the ward, hiding behind a door, waiting for a nurse on the desk to be called away. I got to the ground floor, using the stairs, not the lift. Strangely enough, there wasn't a reception on the ground floor in this section of the hospital, so I made my way out and called a taxi to Ash Hall.

I found myself staggering into the Bridle Path alongside the nursing home. I had to rest. The sleep drug was taking control again. I don't know what she had given me, but probably Diazepam. That's probably why I was feeling dizzy, uncoordinated and sick. One of its side-effects was hallucinations. I also had a blazing headache.

I kept repeating to myself, "I've got to get back, I've got to get back, I've got to get back."…. then remembered no more.

CHAPTER 13

Wek up Jane, com an. Thah's trubble at th'ouse". I opened my eyes. John was standing over me. We were on the Bridle Path and there was a roaring commotion of a number of raised voices, coming from Ash Hall. "Sounds like the mob has got here, John."

"Indayed, God 'elp us." And he started to run down Bridle Path to get to the entrance of Ash Hall. Something told me to stop him and I shouted out after him. "John, come back, you're heading into trouble, get back here. You're way out of your depth."

He didn't stop and disappeared around the corner. I knew I shouldn't follow him. Something had startled me, an idea, an image and I was fixed rigid to the spot - I couldn't move. John running away, recalled to mind the figure I had seen running away from the nursing home, just before I was brought back in time. That person had the same form and shape and gait as John, who I had just seen running away. The person I had seen running was John!

I looked through the hedge, where I could just about see a group of people, shouting and haranguing Job Meigh. They were obviously still livid following their treatment in Burslem. They still had fire in their hearts and the rain hadn't dampened their spirits.

It looked like Job Meigh had been warned of their approach as they'd marched up Ash Bank. He was standing on the steps in front of the Hall. I then saw John making his way up the steps to Mr Meigh. They shook hands and Mr Meigh clapped John on the back. The door was half open and from my viewpoint I could see, through the window as the curtains had been left open, Joseph Weston, the coachman, placing hats, cloaks and coats on chairs and wherever in that front room – one coat after another – I didn't know where they were all coming from. Maybe Mr Meigh had guests and he'd asked for the coats to be hung on backs of chairs to dry after the downpour. I couldn't work it out.

Mr Meigh was having an argument with people in the crowd. They were stating their demands and Mr Meigh was refuting them, giving examples of his own generosity towards his workforce.

Theirs were the demands that we had heard earlier in Burslem, more money, food, a decent living and so on. "I state to you beseechingly that the people who worked for me have found me to be a man who has looked after his workers. Yes, I have a luxurious lifestyle in comparison to your own, as have most other pottery owners, but not at the expense of my workers, I am not one of those. I have looked after my workers. I have provided sickness benefits for them. I have made sure they had dwellings. I have made sure they had regular work so they could earn enough to feed their families."

"Yer still filthy reech, en cayre nowt fer the loiks ef us."

and similar cries were being shouted out as Mr Meigh tried to state his case.

I then heard John's voice rise above the tumult, "Mr Meigh's a fayre mon. 'Es don alreet ba may. E looked efter may when ah woz seek en codna wark. E luks efter all ef 'is payple. 'E's a good mon. Git going whom. Yar've turned an the rang one 'ere."

Someone shouted from the crowd, "Whut yer gonna day – fayt all on us, bay yerseln?"

Claim and counter-claim, challenge and rebuttal, allegation and refutation flowed to and fro in a noisy torrent. It looked like, whatever he said, Mr Meigh, with or without John's back-up, was not going to win the argument. They were out for blood and I didn't know what was holding them back. I'd heard talk of a secret tunnel leading under the Hall to Ash House over the main road. I didn't know if it existed but I couldn't see Mr Meigh getting out of this one – but then again, I couldn't see him running and letting his lovely new Hall get burnt to the ground as they had done with so many other buildings.

Mr Meigh continued, "I've even taken it upon myself to look into the toxins present in the paintwork used on my pots. I have carried out copious research into this, all to prevent my workforce from suffering needlessly from poisons contained in them. I don't know if you've seen in the grounds but there are small pools along the stream, and a water wheel. There I have mixed the colours and tested them. These trials have been tested and manufacturers only use these new glazes now. This has been my work, to aid all pottery workers, to prevent them from having to ingest poisonous substances either through the skin or breathing in toxins.

Mr Meigh was trying to edge the crowd further around towards the windows of the front-facing room.

Just then someone shouted out. He'd seen the outdoor raiments apparently drying in that front room., "Hay lads, owd up, hay's got a bliddy army in theer. Ay's trying te trick us." The mob paused, its resolution broke, its solidarity crumbled and away it began to drift, slowly and then with increasing rapidity as rain drops, once more, began to blow over Ash Bank.

"Have you seen Jane?" Mr Meigh asked John.

"Why, shay woz wi may a moment ago….. Shay's no well." I could sense John trying to work out what to say, hedging his bets, trying to get an idea of what Mr Meigh knew.

"I'm angry with her. She's left my wife all on her own, to fend for herself, with no offer of assistance, so she could not leave her room."

John was thinking on the spot now, "Ah'm sorry, suur, but shay's no bin well all daay. Shay's running a fayver. Ah'm sorry ah codna git te Mrs Meigh."

He went inside for a second and came out with a load of leaflets and papers that we'd picked up on our visits to the Chartist meetings. He threw them at him "So, you're nothing to do with these rioters and so-called Chartists? I found them in your rooms?"

"Thay war fer me bruther in Tunster. Way went thah to veesit as Jane wanted te nay mer abut the Charteests but way've ed nowt te day wi thayse rioters. Way've bin 'ere al-toim."

"So, where is Jane?"

John had to think quickly again. Where was I meant to be all this time, so very sick?

"Shay's bin owt bek int' jetty, caught bad, tisicky. Ah gor wit flannels fer ar yed. Clayned har up, geen har somink te drank. Ah thenk shay's fallen aslayp now."

"So, you haven't been near Burslem today, it's just that someone looking very much like Jane has been seen there, among the rioters?"

"No, sur, certaynly not, sur – most 'ev bin someun oo luks layk har – mistayken identity loik."

"And what have you done to your hand, John. I see it is bandaged?"

"Oo, ah coot mesel, oot chopping wood. Nor much but mayns ah evna bin able te do much labouring, loik, en ah wodna 'ev bin able te 'elp Mrs Meigh dinestairs."

"That sounds reasonable, John. I see you've been busy with Jane. I was worried you had forsaken me and joined these rioters – and that after all I did for when your work suffered at the factory after the death of your wife.

Anyway, I'm sure Dinah can provide Jane with some tonic or other, then she should be put to bed. I'm sure you can see to that between you." At this point they went inside. I took the opportunity to run round, skirting under the windows, to the back outhouse toilet. Where I positioned myself on the floor, feigning sleep, although this did not take much effort.

Soon John appeared, calling my name, "I'm here, John, in the outhouse."

"Good, I'll go and fetch Dinah."

Dinah gave me some form of linctus and John carried

me to my room. Dinah then said she'd go make me some chamomile and ginger tea, which would help my headache.

"John," I murmured, "I did not want this all to end like this. You've been brilliant. A Godsend. I've never known anyone like you. I've put you into so much trouble, almost got you killed." I struggled to sit up and gave him a hug, resting my head into his chest and John put his arms around me.

"Dinna tok loik thut, ducky. Ah dinna day onything ah didna want te day. Donna mither yersen."

"I really believe that Mr Meigh, if he'd known the truth about today, and if he had seen us together, it would have sent him over the top. You know he has made advances to me. I believe he would have gone into a jealous rage and I don't think it is beyond him to have taken his rage out on you, on both of us, physically."

"Yer, ah 'ad to think sharpshins, put on't spot az ah wuz, 'specially when 'e produced those Charteest pamphlets. A mite cunny-fogle. Ah wuz afreared ah wud bay fanged out."

"You're such a lovely man, John. In fact I think I've fallen in love with you. I don't ever want to leave you but I'm not sure if I can stay." I did not want to think about it but, what if this was all a dream, an hallucination brought on by the Diazepam? What if I was whisked back to my own time again and had to leave the love of my life.

"Whut de yer mayn? Geev over, Ah want yer te stay, Jane. Ah belayve thar knowst ah love ye too." He kissed me, tenderly. "Eef you'll 'av may, ah wanna wed ye. Wun yer marry may, Jane? Way con fend fer oorsel – git away fer 'ere en Mr Meigh, day a flit."

"Yes, of course I'll marry you, John. You're everything

to me. You're the kindest person I've ever known and I know you'd give your life to protect me." We held hands, as John sat on the bed next to me.

At that moment Dinah came in with the tea. "You look cosy there, both of yers. What's 'appened?"

"Dinah," I replied rather excitedly, "John and I are going to be married."

"Well, be Jesus. That's a turn-up for the books. That's come out o' the blue. But, you'll 'av to tell the master. Don't know what 'e'll think of it all."

"Is there any way we can keep it secret from him, just put in our notices and just go?"

"Nay ducky. No good keeping secrets. They allus come out in the wash.

Just then the room seemed to start spinning. At first I thought it was the stress of having to tell Job Meigh and my headache but then my eyesight started to fade. John and Dinah were fading away before my eyes. "John, hold onto me, John. Don't let me go." I screamed.

I could feel his arms around me but everything was going black.

"**I want to stay**" I started shouting over and over again, "**Let me stay, I don't want to go back.**"

"She's coming round," I heard vaguely. The voice was coming from a far off place, blowing in on the breeze. "Jane, Jane". I heard someone calling me from what seemed like an island, so far away, drowned out by the foaming sea breaking against the rocks.

"Oh doctor, I thought she was dead." The first voice said, "She's been unawares for a couple of days now."

"Yes, she's been unconscious. However, her pulse is

getting stronger, which is a good sign." I could sense a light in my eyes and tried to blink but there was pressure on my eyelids. "Her irises are reacting to the light, which is another good sign."

"I believe she must have suffered a great shock of some kind, something her mind could not fathom, something that would have killed off someone not as strong, especially being so weak from lack of sustenance and fluids. Her body just shut down. I've put her on intravenous fluids, as you can see from the tube I've inserted into her arm and the drip bag. It is a system of replacing lost body fluids developed by Dr Thomas Latta of Leith. Mr Meigh was very lucky to get hold of me, as I am one of the few doing studies into this system, and my time is precious. Mr Meigh is a very generous and persuasive man. I believe our young lady would have died without my intervention."

"Look, she's moved her head slightly." A man said.

"Jane, Jane" and I could feel someone clinging onto my hand. "Com bek te may, Jane."

"What, what did he say" I found myself pondering, "something like 'com bek te may'. It was a strong accent. Did he mean, 'come back to me'?"

It couldn't be, could it? No, my prayers wouldn't have been answered. I must still be in hospital…. Was that John? No, it would probably be a male nurse or someone else from the Potteries. I daren't open my eyes. I was too scared to. I didn't want the horrible disappointment of finding myself back in the 21st century. I wanted my John, my lovely John. I started to cry.

"Look, shay's weeping. Doctor, shay moost bay in payne. Day someink, playse."

"I've given her some Laudanum to give her some relief, she should be coming round soon."

"Jane, Jane, ah'm 'ere fer ye. Yer safe neow. Eet's may, John. Wayke oop, playse."

The voice sounded like John's and he said, 'It's me, John'. Am I dead? Am I alive? What year am I in? Should I try to open my eyes? I'm scared.

"Thar's nothing te bay afeared ef – ah'm 'ere. Com an – open yer ayze. Thut's may girl – may wife te bay."

It is John, he's calling me his wife to be. "John." I heard myself say, barely audibly.

"Thut's eet, Jane. Eet's may, John. Yer con day eet. Open yer ayze."

One eye flickered. I can do this, I can. I closed it again quickly. Everything was too bright. I shook my head and found my hand going up to my eyes.

"Dim the lights, close the curtains." I heard someone say, presumably a doctor. The blinding light that was visible through my closed eyelids, faded. I tried again to open my eyes.

There was John, kneeling beside the bed, holding onto my other hand. He looked like he'd been crying. His eyes were red and his face tear-stained. I grabbed his hand. "It's good to be back." I managed to get out. My voice was hoarse. John reached over and gave me a hug and kisses all over my face.

"Eet's gud te 'ev ye back, darling girl."

My dimmed eyesight managed to make out other figures in the room. I saw what, presumably, was a doctor, in a dark suit and top hat with something that looked like a stethoscope around his neck, but having only one ear-piece.

Behind him were Dinah and Mr Meigh. I was startled to see Mr Meigh there. He must now know that John had proposed to me. What must his thoughts be, after he had made such advances towards me? Was he angry – he didn't look so? I could see a look of tenderness and worry in his eyes.

"Mr Meigh, sir."

"It is alright, Jane. Do not try to speak. I know you are very weak. We have all been extremely worried about you, especially John, and we are all so very pleased to have you back in our lives. John has told me he has proposed and you have accepted. I am very pleased for you both. John is a good man. He's explained everything that happened. You have nothing to worry about." He then bent over towards me and whispered, "I would have liked a different future for you, as you know, but that was just wishful-thinking – something I knew could never be. I am extremely sorry for causing you distress." He then straightened up and spoke so everyone could hear. "Jane", and turning to John, "I will make sure you have a cottage for your future abode together."

"Thank you very much, sir. I am extremely grateful." I managed to say, before falling asleep again.

So, everything was going to be fine. I was back in 1842, with my beloved John, and it looked like I was going to stay. I don't know how that happened. I shouldn't be there. It was a miracle. A miracle brought about by love. What happened to me back in the 21st century, I've no idea? I must have been dying on the Bridle Path – there was no way I could be in two places, so my spirit just drifted back to 1842. Either that, or this was all an hallucination that never happened and I remained in the 21st century to bury John's bones. Take your pick.

What I did find out was that there was a Rosalind Paget, who was one of four nurses, who founded the Chartered Society of Physiotherapy in 1894. Maybe a daughter carried on Jane's work, wishing to carry on her mother's name, in remembrance of the work her mother has started.

Maybe, maybe not.

SAMPLE NEWSPAPER REPORTS FOLLOWING THE RIOTS

17 August – Shipping and Mercantile Gazette, London

"... shortly afterward a detachment of the 21 Dragoon Guards headed by R Adderley and Job Meigh Esqs., two country magistrates, arrived. Upwards of 20 individuals, chiefly in state of stupid intoxication, were immediately..."

19 August – Durham County Advertiser

".... Fire and that very alarming riots were going on in the neighbourhood. The magistrates sitting at Burslem (Mr Adderley and Mr Job Meigh) immediately ordered both the infantry and dragoons to proceed to the scene of disturbance (half past seven).

20 August – The Suffolk Chronicle

"hall burnt early this morning in the north of this county. It is reported that the new and beautiful mansion belonging to Job Meigh was ransomed from destruction early this morning for the sum of £20, although this is not given as fact.

22 August – London Observer

"The infantry were quartered in the Town Hall, but about three o'clock an express arrived from Lane-end setting the Town Hall on fire, and that very alarming riots were going on in the neighbourhood. The insurgents at Burslem (Mr Adderley and Mr Job Meigh) immediately ordered both the infantry and dragoons to proceed to the scene of disturbance...."

23 August – Kentish Gazette

".... On fire and that very alarming riots were going on in the neighbourhood. The magistrates (\Mr Adderley and Mr Job Meigh) immediately ordered both the infantry and dragoons to proceed to the scene of disturbance, and up to the present hour..."

31 December – Staffordshire Advertiser

Hanley: sat down to an excellent dinner at the Hall Inn, Werrington. The dinner was given by the Rev C S Hassels and Job Meigh, Esq, as a mark of their approbation of the energy and zeal manifested by the special constable force of the direct."

Longton

In the early 18th century Longton was a 'rude scattered hamlet without form. In the 19th century, when the town began to develop, the science of planning was unknown. Development was haphazard and the borough's shape determined by commercial considerations alone. Robert Slaney looked into the sanitary regulations and cleanliness. There was a plentiful and cheap water supply from and natural drainage was good. Public lighting was one of the first areas to be improved, as a matter of security. From 1835 the British Gas Light Company provided gas lighting. Longton's courts and alleys was deemed 'a nuisance', embracing all forms of noxious accumulations, especially great piles of human sewage stacked by the roadside or in a courtyard - small houses, very bad open privies, refuse in heaps; puddles (probably urine) – an annual mortality rate of 2.7%. A house of £15 per annum rental has a small back yard, washhouse, water and a privy with covered ash-place but no drainage. One passage has no drain but the refuse thrown down drains into the walls and foundations. The street is only sewered half its length. Privies open out into the street. The cellars have water in them.

The working man, returning to his home, which is often surrounded by detritus, with no provision for drainage or cleansing, affected by the smell and having no water for his use, readily resorts to the spirit shop or public house. The woman, neglected and peevish, visits her vexation on her children or husband. Amid such scenes the children become hardened, careless of cleanliness, unused to order; and all the benefit from the best education which may be given is destroyed by the constant evil examples they see around their homes.

In 1848, following a rapid spread of cholera there was a move to undertake an enquiry preliminary to the adoption of the 1848 Public Health Act but Longton and the potters of Hanley and Shelton opposed this. They could not afford to pay for a more healthy environment and they were frightened of anyone who might force them into a standard of living they could not afford.

Cinder heaps, sometimes six feet above the level of the house doors, cesspools overflowing onto the pavement, constant smoke, in-town pigsties and stagnant open ditches.

In 1935 there were still houses described as miserable single-roomed windowless huts, sometimes occupied by as many as eight persons – one house in 1842 accommodated 15 persons.

Wage levels 15-16s a week for a general labourer – rents normally £2-3 a year.

Law and Order

In 1930 a police force for the southern part of the potteries was created. This very act was provocative with a mob responding immediately to test out the new force. The police were assaulted with stones and other missiles. Captains Tomlinson and Mainwaring, Lieutenant Adderley and the military arrested the mob and they were taken to Newcastle but the mob still attacked, this time with the use of fire arms, so the military were ordered to respond in like kind. This was mainly caused by elections with conservative candidates being attacked. The threshold of violence was higher than today and could easily be lifted to the level of communal riot by the intrusion of an event like an election, or by pressure of bad harvests or a down turn in trade.

The common people used what seemed the only weapon available to them: ranged against them was the coercion of long hours of employment in bad conditions for a pitifully low wage, a sense of exclusion from being able to take part in determining their future, and deaf ears to their distress. Only men with property could vote.

Pottery Riots 1842 - Researched by John Lumsdon

For the first time, many thousands of workers' acted together, creating unity, cohesion, and a feeling of common interest that provided a basis for building working class organisations. The United Branches of Operative Potters (UBOP) was born on the 6th of September 1843 Likewise the Cotton Spinners Association. And the Operative Stonemasons' membership swelled from 2,134 in 1842 to 4,861 in 1845. The printing trades united to form the National Typographical Association and the Tailors and Shoemakers where in the process of forming national societies. The powerful United Flint Glass Makers' Society was strong enough to withstand a legal onslaught that cost them £1,800, and it was in this context of emerging trade unionism that the Miners' association of Great Britain and Ireland was born.

https://www.tameside.gov.uk/tmbc_images/include/bp_strike2.jpg

The General Strike

The general strike itself was a cry of despair from the whole of the country. Economic conditions had deteriorated: unemployment was extensive, in some towns reaching as much as half the population, whilst those fortunate enough to be employed were often on short time, and subject to frequent wage cuts. Almost all of the working class was on the verge of starvation In a Midlands' miners' report it stated - "They did not mind being hungry themselves, but when they heard their wives and children crying for bread, it cut them through and they could not stand it". They talked of walking to London to see the Queen and Prime Minister for they thought the sight of a long column, marching six a breast would be impressive. They believed that affairs in London were in some mysterious way the source of their problems. The background to events in the Potteries was similar to that elsewhere. It had been severely hit by the depression: the workhouses were overcrowded; prices were high and wage cuts frequent.

The weight of Queen Victoria's influence was thrown on the side of energetic repression. The Queen's orders were carried out with savage vengeance for the burning down of the Rev Dr Vale's house. He was the vicar of St James's Church on Uttoxeter Road and also a coal owner. Six men were transported to Australia for 21 years each, and sentences were passed on others for complicity in the same offence. A total of 189 years imprisonment was imposed, and, for pillaging and burning the Rev. Aitkin's home, terms of imprisonment totalling 93 years were imposed.

Some, who had taken no part in the riots, were arrested.

One of these was Joseph Capper, a well-known Chartist Methodist local preacher. His arrest took place on the Sunday evening of August 21st, 1842 following the riots of August 15th- 16th. At the meeting of the 15th on Crown Bank Hanley, Capper had urged the people resolutely but peaceably to seek their rights. From there he went back to the anvil in his blacksmith's shop and worked all the week.

On Sunday evening he was reading his bible to his wife, son and daughter, who were joining him in the family worship, when four men burst into his house unceremoniously and seized him saying, "You are the man we want Joseph Capper". Then his son, a big lad like his dad, swung a fist and laid one of the men on the floor, but a quiet word from his father probably prevented the other three following him. Capper was arrested, tried and sentenced to two years' imprisonment in Stafford gaol for sedition.

He came out broken down in health due to prison food and environment, but strong as ever in the consciousness of his integrity. He was met by friends and went on his way home through the Potteries triumphantly applauded by thousands of people who believed in his perfect innocence. About the unfairness of the administration of the law, many liberals and humanitarians where appalled by the severity with which the authorities dealt anyone remotely connected with the disturbances.

The final result of the strike was far from what the employers anticipated.

They found themselves unable to impose the large-scale wage reductions (sometimes as much as 25 per cent) that they had originally intended, and the workers drew the lesson that by their efforts and through their strike they had gained at least a partial victory, a powerful impetus was given towards the creation of trade unions.

The Miners' Association of Great Britain and Ireland was formally established at Wakefield on the 7th November 1842 and constitutes an important landmark in the history of British trade unions. Its size, structure and intention made it in many ways the prototype of modern trade unions, an advance on previous combinations of workmen, which flourished for a while, then were smashed.

In North Staffs, unlike some other coalfields, the coal owners did not make a determined attempt to crush the unions. Perhaps, they wished to avoid a repetition of the orgy and violence that occurred during the general strike for some had still not made good their losses. Lord Granvile's pits at Shelton had employed 300 men in 1842 but two of his furnaces had been blown up and not replaced and now only 100 were employed. Doubtless, with this in mind, the North Staffs coal trade met in December, and, after a long discussion, decided to tolerate the existence of the Miners' Association in the coalfield. In December 1843, the Shelton miners, many of them not in the union, went on strike and won a wage increase.

The Association held a national conference in the Temperance Hall in Burslem from the 15th to 19th July 1844, and the conference decided to hire the service of a legal advisor by the name of W.P.Roberts. He was known as the miners' attorney. This was for the whole of the association and each member contributed a half penny to the maintenance of a legal department. Roberts defended miners in court but, on many occasions, he knew he did not have a chance of winning, as it was the law that needed changing. Unfortunately, there was no one in parliament who would change laws for the benefit of the working class. At this same conference, at the instigation of the Bury district, the union established a general fund. In the first instance this was to help the northeast miners who were on strike, but, later for the support of all miners on strike.

An important function of the Burslem conference was to hold an intensive campaign in North Staffs in an attempt to restore the local union organisation to health. Public meetings were held in Hanley, Smallthorne, Knutton, Alsagers Bank, Longton and Tunstall with W.P.Roberts as the main speaker and including W.Dixson, J.Lomax, H.Birrell, J.Taylor, B.Watson C.Parkinson and T.Weaver, but, as there were 4,000 miners in North Staffs nearly 1,000 of whom were permanently unemployed, it was hardly surprising the union remained weak and in a poor bargaining position. However, this was the start of permanent trade unions.

AFTERMATH

Queen Victoria herself was worried. She wrote to Sir Robert Peel, the Prime Minister, that she was surprised at the little or no opposition to the dreadful riots in the Potteries and the passiveness of the troops. She said they ought to act and meetings ought to be prevented. Everything should be done to apprehend Cooper and all his delegates who were members of the Chartist movement, an organisation trying to reform the political system. The six objects of their charter, five of which we take for granted today, were;

1. Universal suffrage.
2. Vote by ballot.
3. Annual parliaments.
4. No property qualifications for MPs.
5. Payments of representatives.
6. Equal electoral districts.

The weight of Queen Victoria's influence was thrown on the side of energetic repression. The Queen's orders were carried out with savage vengeance for the burning down of the Rev Dr Vale's house. He was the vicar of St James's Church on Uttoxeter Road and also a coal owner.

Six men were transported to Australia for 21 years each, and sentences were passed on others for complicity in the same offence. A total of 189 years imprisonment was imposed, and, for pillaging and burning the Rev. Aitkin's home, terms of imprisonment totalling 93 years were imposed.

Some, who had taken no part in the riots, were arrested. One of these was Joseph Capper, a well-known Chartist Methodist local preacher. His arrest took place on the Sunday evening of August 21st, 1842 following the riots of August 15th- 16th. At the meeting of the 15th on Crown Bank Hanley, Capper had urged the people resolutely but peaceably to seek their rights. From there he went back to the anvil in his blacksmith's shop and worked all the week.

On Sunday evening he was reading his bible to his wife, son and daughter, who were joining him in the family worship, when four men burst into his house unceremoniously and seized him saying, "You are the man we want Joseph Capper".

Then his son, a big lad like his dad, swung a fist and laid one of the men on the floor, but a quiet word from his father probably prevented the other three following him.

Capper was arrested, tried and sentenced to two years' imprisonment in Stafford gaol for sedition. He came out broken down in health due to prison food and environment, but strong as ever in the consciousness of his integrity.

He was met by friends and went on his way home through the Potteries triumphantly applauded by thousands of people who believed in his perfect innocence. About the unfairness of the administration of the law, many liberals and humanitarians where appalled by the severity with which the authorities dealt anyone remotely connected with the disturbances.

However, the draconian punishment meted out had a profound effect on the working class. A bond of suffering united them with brothers in other parts of the country, and thus the repression helped to develop a feeling of class-consciousness. This was especially true among miners who bore the brunt of the strike its self and many gaol sentences. As a result, when miners heard of their fellow miners from other coalfields being arrested and imprisoned, they did not regard this as a matter of no concern to themselves. They held protest meetings and collected money for the victims.

The miners, whether of coal or metal, were an isolated body of men often separated geographically from the rest of working people and concerned themselves more with their economic struggles than the Chartist agitators. Nevertheless, throughout 1842, the 'Northern Star' contained the nominations to the Chartist General Council, and from it we find the north-east miners were strong supporters of Chartism, and, interestingly that there were five North Staffs' miners nominated, including George Hemmings and Thomas Mayer who were local leaders of the general strike in the summer of 1842.

The final result of the strike was far from what the employers anticipated. They found themselves unable to impose the large-scale wage reductions (sometimes as much as 25 per cent) that they had originally intended, and the workers drew the lesson that by their efforts and through their strike they had gained at least a partial victory, a powerful impetus was given towards the creation of trade unions.

The Miners' Association of Great Britain and Ireland was formally established at Wakefield on the 7th November 1842 and constitutes an important landmark in the history of British trade unions. Its size, structure and intention made it in many ways the prototype of modern trade unions, an advance on previous combinations of workmen, which flourished for a while, then were smashed.

In North Staffs, unlike some other coalfields, the coal owners did not make a determined attempt to crush the unions. Perhaps, they wished to avoid a repetition of the orgy and violence that occurred during the general strike for some had still not made good their losses. Lord Granvile's pits at Shelton had employed 300 men in 1842 but two of his furnaces had been blown up and not replaced and now only 100 were employed. Doubtless, with this in mind, the North Staffs coal trade met in December, and, after a long discussion, decided to tolerate the existence of the Miners' Association in the coalfield. In December 1843, the Shelton miners, many of them not in the union, went on strike and won a wage increase.

The Association held a national conference in the Temperance Hall in Burslem from the 15th to 19th July 1844, and the conference decided to hire the service of a legal advisor by the name of W.P.Roberts. He was known as the miners' attorney. This was for the whole of the association and each member contributed a half penny to the maintenance of a legal department. Roberts defended miners in court but, on many occasions, he knew he did not have a chance of winning, as it was the law that needed changing. Unfortunately, there was no one in parliament who would change laws for the benefit of the working class.

At this same conference, at the instigation of the Bury district, the union established a general fund. In the first instance this was to help the northeast miners who were on strike, but, later for the support of all miners on strike.

An important function of the Burslem conference was to hold an intensive campaign in North Staffs in an attempt to restore the local union organisation to health. Public meetings were held in Hanley, Smallthorne, Knutton, Alsagers Bank, Longton and Tunstall with W.P.Roberts as the main speaker and including W.Dixson, J.Lomax, H.Birrell, J.Taylor, B.Watson C.Parkinson and T.Weaver, but, as there were 4,000 miners in North Staffs nearly 1,000 of whom were permanently unemployed, it was hardly surprising the union remained weak and in a poor bargaining position. However, this was the start of permanent trade unions.

EVENTUAL REFORMS

Chartism did not directly generate any reforms. It was not until 1867 that urban working men were admitted to the franchise under the Reform Act 1867, and not until 1918 that full manhood suffrage was achieved. Slowly the other points of the People's Charter were granted: secret voting was introduced in 1872 and the payment of MPs under the Parliament Act of 1911. Annual elections remain the only Chartist demand not to be implemented. Participation in the Chartist Movement filled some working men with self-confidence: they learned to speak publicly, to send their poems and other writings off for publication, to be able, in short, to confidently articulate the feelings of working people. Many former Chartists went on to become journalists, poets, ministers, and councillors. Political elites feared the Chartists in the 1830s and 1840s as a dangerous threat to national stability. In the Chartist stronghold of Manchester, the reform movement undermined the political power of the old Tory-Anglican elite that had controlled civic affairs. However, the reformers of Manchester were themselves factionalised.

After 1848, as the movement faded, its demands appeared less threatening and were gradually enacted by other reformers. After 1848, middle class parliamentary Radicals continued to press for an extension of the franchise in such organisations as the National Parliamentary and Financial Reform Association and the Reform Union. By the late 1850s, the celebrated John Bright was agitating in the country for franchise reform. However, working class radicals had not gone away. The Reform League campaigned for manhood suffrage in the 1860s, and included former Chartists amongst its ranks. Chartism has also been regarded by historians as a forerunner to the UK Labour Party.

NOTES

Note 1:

The first factory reform act was passed in 1802 but it was not until 1840 that Dr Samuel Scriven was appointed by the House of Commons to investigate and report on the 'Employment' of Children and Young Persons in the District of the North Staffordshire Potteries and on the Actual State, conditions and Treatment of Such Children and Young Persons'.

His report, which contained site visits and numerous interviews with children, found youngsters toiling in appalling conditions.

His report, published in 1843, found. The class of children whose physical condition has the strongest claims to consideration is that of the 'jiggers' and 'mould-runners' who, by the very nature of their work, are rendered pale, were diminutive and unhealthy; they are employed by the dish, saucer, and plate makers; their hours are half past five in the morning to six at night, but in numberless instances they are required to labour on to eight, nine or ten, and thisin an atmosphere varying from 100 to 120 degrees, all these extra hours being occasioned, nine times out of ten, by the selfishness or irregularities of their unworthy taskmaster.

As a result of the investigation, Parliament passed legislation controlling the hours and conditions of work for young people.

However, unlike the coal mines and textile mills, the Staffordshire pottery industry was not named in the new acts because, despite the hard life endured by children, most post-banks actually offered better conditions than the minimum required by the new law.

Note 2:

Voting was not made secret until 1871.

Note 3:

The charter was launched in Glasgow in May 1838, at a meeting attended by an estimated 150,000 people. Presented as a popular-style Magna Carta, it rapidly gained support across the country and its supporters became known as the Chartists. A petition, populated at the Chartist meetings across Britain, was brought to London in May 1939, for MP Thomas Attwood to present to Parliament. It boasted 1,280,958 signatures, yet Parliament voted not to consider it. However, the Chartists continued to campaign for the six points of the Charter for many years to come, and produced two more petitions to Parliament.

02 May 1842 vol 62 cc1373-811373

A Petition from the working classes throughout the kingdom, of the presentation of which Mr. Thomas Duncombe had previously given notice, was brought down to the House, by a procession consisting of a vast multitude. Its bulk was so great, that the doors were not wide enough to admit it, and it was necessary to unroll it, to carry it into the House. When unrolled, it spread over a great part of the floor, and rose above the level of the Table.

Note 4:

The Peterloo Massacre of 16 August 1819 was the result of a cavalry charge into the crowd at a public meeting at Saint Peters Field, in Manchester, England. Eleven people were killed and more than 400, including many women and children, injured. Local magistrates arranged for a substantial number of regular soldiers to be on hand. The troops included 600 men of the 15th Hussars; several hundred infantrymen; a Royal Horse Artillery unit with two six-pounder (2.7 kg) guns; 400 men of the Cheshire Yeomanry, 400 special constables and 120 cavalry of the Manchester and Salford Yeomanry, relatively inexperienced militia recruited from among shopkeepers and tradesmen.[

Note 5:

This plaque was put up in Burslem in April 2018 to commemorate the young boy murdered in the riots on 16 August 1842 outside the Big House.

Heapy was 19 years old and born in Quarnford, Staffordshire. He was an orphan. His mother had died when he was 3 years old and his father when he was 11 years old. He moved to Leek and worked as a shoe maker. [9] Heapy was shot in the head in front of the "Big House" on Moorland Road and died instantly. [10] [11]

Josiah Heapy's funeral was arranged at St. Edward's, Leek on 18th August and apparently led to no disorder. Although there has been local speculation, the location of his grave has not been found.[12]. A verdict of Justifiable Homicide was given. [13]

SENTENCING

From Bradford alone, there were between four and five thousand marchers. The end came at Burslem, where the crowd was forcibly dispersed by dragoons and special constables. One man was killed when the troops fired into the crowd; several were seriously wounded. Almost as suddenly as it had begun, the unrest was over.

In the aftermath, the Potteries towns were placed, as the Northern Star's reporter put it, under "martial law.... Absolute despotism is practiced upon us" (Fyson, p. 212). Staffordshire Chartist leader John Richards called it a "Tory reign of Terror" as, in the two weeks from October 1 to 15, 218 men and women from North Staffordshire were put on trial plus 56 from South Staffordshire. 146 were given sentences ranging from 2 months to 2 years (these figures increased over the next 2 years as more people were caught and tried.

The chief judge was Sir Nicholas Tindall, Lord Chief Justice of Common Please; most were tried in groups of up to 30 at a time, making errors and false identification by witnesses all the more likely.

The minors suffered badly with about 19 transported and 17 jailed.

As for the potters – about 21 were transported and 67 jailed.

Of the women, 23 were tried, 14 found guilty

46-year-old Ann Mewis was give 8 months with hard labour.

Cooper, who had tried to escape before the riots of 16th August, was narrowly acquitted on a charge of arson, escaping transportation. Immediately thereafter, he was indicted for seditious conspiracy for the "Slaves, toil no more!" speech. The indictment alleged that Cooper, along with John Richards and another local Chartist, Joseph Cappur,

Wllliam Garrett, shot in the back at Burslem, was sentenced to 2 years hard labour despite being in convalescence from his wounds.

John Ashley, a master tailor from Newcastle. No crime other than he stopped in the street to watch Rose's house being burnt, was sentenced to 12 months hard labour. Both William Garrett and John Ashley died in Millbank Penitentiary in London serving their sentences.

Thomas Adkins, was taken to Newcastle for imprisonment on 14th August, where he died. At the inquest held by the Coroner, Mr Stanier, a couple of days later, it was stated that death was due to drinking to excess. His brain had been turned to alcohol, according to the surgeon, Mr Tail, who had carried out the Post Mortem.

George Colclough, alias Cogsey Nelly, aka Cogzynelly, aka Joe Bowley, a 21-year-old minor, was sentenced to 21 years transportation – charged with riot, attempting to demolish Forrester's house, setting fire to Parker's and Vale's, and demanding money with threats from the landlord of the

George, Burslem. He was to return to England from Van Diemen's Land, and by 1868 had set up as a shopkeeper. He played no part in any local politics ever again.

Richard Croxton was sentenced to transportation. In Van Diemen's Land he committed a long string of crimes, which led to his ticket being revoked in 1858.

John Neal, "Chartist's Home Secretary", left prison after 2 years hard labour. He was reported to be in very poor health.

William Plan, 23-years-old, was sentenced to two weeks' hard labour, for intimidating a woman into parting with a shipping.

Mary Hall, landlady of the George and Dragon, New Street, lost her liquor licence for holding Chartist meetings.

Thomas Owen, a labourer from Shelton, was committed for trial, charged with rioting at Rev Aitkins property.

Edward Smith, a clog pattern maker, was committed for trial, charged with riot and feloniously destroying property at Dr Vale's house.

Elizabeth Poulson and Samuel Wilshaw were charged with stealing pledges from Mr Hall, pawnbroker at Hanley, on 16th – these pledges were later returned so both were discharged.

Adam Wood was committed for trial, charged with riot and stealing several plated candlesticks from Rev Aitkins.

Samuel Tildsley was committed for trial, charged with breaking the windows in Burslem Town Hall on 6th August

Richard Croxton was accused of taking seven sovereigns from Mr Meigh's foreman, by intimidation and stating that he was "walking up to his knees in blood", which did not impress the magistrates!

Dennis Mulligan was charged with stealing. In a broad Irish accent he was quoted as saying, "It was not a glass I was drinking out of, gentlemen, it was a bacon dish!"

Thomas Lester charged for inciting violence

Ten men and women were charged with rioting and demolishing property at Dr Vale's on 15th.

Richard Wright was charged with setting fire to the house with a firebrand, which he applied to a heap of broken furniture in one of Dr Vale's rooms.

He, along with Thomas Jackson, William Hollins and Mary Shaw were charged with throwing furniture on a fire in front of Dr Vale's.

James Earp was charged for demolishing the woodwork around the windows at Dr Vales'.

Joseph and Philip Saunders were charged with breaking bedroom furniture by banging the pieces together.

Rosanna Ellis and Milllicent Saunders were charged with stealing alcohol

Elizabeth Robinson was charged with stealing clothes.

Jeremiah Yates, potter and keeper of a coffee shop near Miles Bank, was charged with turning out the workmen at the factory of Messrs. Ridgway, Morley & Co, in Shelton on 15th, and sent for trial.

ACKNOWLEDGEMENTS

When I was a Child – by Charles Shaw **Excerpt from John Abberley and his book "Salute to the Potters" printed in The Sentinel, Monday, January 16 2017:**

Walk Around Stoke – from your computer - www. thepotteries.org – Steve Birks

A Chartist Speak, 1842 – Thomas Cooper

The Purgatory of Suicides: Sedition, Chartism, and Epic Poetry by Thomas Cooper

British Library, The People's Charter

Staffordshire Advertiser, 12 March 1842 and 31 December 1842

Shipping and Mercantile Gazette, London 17 August 1842

Durham Country Advertiser 19 August 1842

Kentish Gazette, Canterbury 23 August 1842

Hampshire Chronicle 22 August 1842

London Observer 22 August 1842

Werrington Library records – History of Stoke on Trent

The Spirit of the Place by M J W Rogers

Turnout of the Colliers in Potteries 1842 – Researched by John Lumsdon

Clayhanger – Arnold Bennett

Fionn Taylor - http://www.healeyhero.co.uk/rescue/New-2018.htm#top2

TRANSLATION FROM POTTERIES DIALECT

Page 29
"There's a place around the back of the stairs, or maybe at the side of the stairs, you know, that will do. I could put up a pulley there, hang it from the ceiling. I'll measure up, see what we can do. It will be a tricky job but I'll have a go dear."

Page 29
"Ah, that would be because I come from the Potteries. Mrs Chetwyn started out the other side of Newcastle. It will come by and by, the more you speak to me."

Page 30
"Yes, I've heard of him. He's not your usual sort of man. I believe he's well respected. If I remember well, it was he who abolished the truck system at his Ubberley pits near Hanley. He paid fair and had a club for sick workers. Yes, he's one of the few good ones."

Pages 101 - 102
"You know that was no accident, neither with Mrs Meigh.

I was there. Don't let on you know or he'll have you guts for garters (he'll string you up)."

"They were having ever such a blazing row the pair of them. Don't know what it was about, wasn't that close up to hear – just heard the noise. Master gets out of the cart, then makes a grab for the Mistress, pulled her right bodily off the cart. Smack on the ground she went, head first and the ground was frozen hard, being February. She lay there some time, not moving. He just walks off. I grabbed her up and took her inside to her room. Dinah tended her but she's never been the same since."

"Where have you been dear? That there is the Potteries. There are hundreds of little potbanks and bottle ovens belching out smoke, choking the very breathe out of everyone there. However, it might be chocking the life out of the workers but it's how folk make a living, put food on the table. The Master had his works down there too. It's not a place for you to be, dear. It's dirty and reeks of humanity, if you know what I mean. I can't say any more to a lady, it wouldn't be right.

Also, there's been something going on down there of late with the coal miners. Early last month 300 coal miners went on strike from Mr Spooner's pits. He cut their wages from 3s 7d a day to just 3s. They cannot live on that. They cannot afford bread to eat and pay their rent. A week or more later, the miners were stopping men from working at the mines. And Lord Shelton's works at Shelton cut wages by 6d a day. Miners and iron workers stopped the engines, pulled the plugs for the boilers. That meant there was no coal, so the pits and potbanks could not be fired, so this led to 5000 workers out on strike. There's been thousands of workers applying for assistance at the work houses every day.

I tell you what, I've got family in Tunstell. I'll take you there and you can talk to them – get some sort of an idea as to what's going on.

Pages 104 - 105
"How are you, dear? Come and sit down" Joan indicated to a chair. "Do you want a saucer of tea? Sorry, but I cannot offer you anything else."

"You'll not be from this area, I can hear".

"Yes, that will be it. What are you doing here?"

"Well, my husband's a coal miner." she pointed to Jimmy. "He's out of work. All the miners are on strike for more money. They've cut their pay and want them to work longer hours. We couldn't live on what he brought home before so they've all come out. We don't know how it will work out. We don't have a pot to piss in now (don't have a penny to our names) and I'm frightened things will just get worse all right. We're clean out of money and starving.

Page 105
The children can talk to you about the work in the potbank. Charlie, Willie, Ann and Lizzie work there. Mary's at school but the older ones are out of work too, as the miners stopped the potbanks working and there's no coal to fire them anyway. If we do not get any money soon, I can see all of us

going to Chell workhouse. Jimmy and I are at our wits end (are lost for ideas and need help).

"Talk to Charlie, he can talk you leg off if you let him (he likes to talk)."

Page 107
"I would have to run in and out of the stove room, winter and summer, with its blazing hot stove. If I was not fast enough, my master would give me what for (reprimand me verbally or physically), because it delayed him in his work and he, in turn, would get reprimanded from his boss, all because of me, and a few times I've been hit and cursed if I was not back in time. I was ill once and could not keep up, had a cold or something and I got such a swipe it knocked me clean off my feet. But I was dripping in sweat and feeling cold at the same time. I was worrying all the time that he would kick the shit out of me or give a leathering."

'Wedging' clay was one of the toughest jobs. "My older brother, Harry, does that job. He's 14. It takes a lot of strength what with him being half-fed, like me, he just does not have the energy" said Charlie.

Page 108
His mother interrupted at this point. "Yes, all of them come back after a day's work, worn out. Our Charlie takes a lunch pack to work but sometimes does not get time to eat it. I make them all porridge but they're almost asleep before finishing it. It's not right. I have to carry them to bed. I just want to cry but we cannot do anything. Father's just not

payed enough and now they have cut his pay. I don't know how we are to manage.

James then cut in, "We'll never survive in the workhouse. They just feed them on greasy water and a few lumps of something that would make a tiger's teeth ache to break the fibres off. I've heard people say it's brutal. They don't feed you enough to live on, just enough to keep you alive. From what I've heard, just a chunk of break and a jug of 'skilly' for supper."

I interrupted, "Sorry, what's skilly, James. I've not come across this term?"

"Well, dear, you never want to. Pig's swill would taste better. It's supposed to be meal and water but it's as thought it's been left to rot before boiling – the violest taste you could ever imagine."

He continued, "There's a school there – boys are hit over the head, over and over if they appear to be slightly slow in learning things. Not that our kids are slow. They can all read."

Pages 109 - 110
"It's not just the miners here that are on strike. We are calling for a general strike all over the country and Scotland and Wales. We'll not go back until they give us more pay. The Chartists have another bill they are going to put before Parliament. They have been preaching all around. Here, have a read of this." Jimmy started shuffling through papers in a drawer and produced a document, which he handed to

me. "This one is from 1838. It will tell you all about what we are fighting for."

Pages 112 - 113
"That's alright, dear. If you are interested, maybe John can take you to one of the Chartist meetings, if you would like that."

"Yes, thank you. Hopefully I'll be able to attend one of them."

Jimmy then turned his attention to the children, "What are you doing lazing about. Get out of here and fetch some coal – get over the moors and get digging and see what else you can steel or cadge, so get going. Take something to dig with, you might find some potatoes or carrots in the farms, but be careful that you are not seen. Keep your heads down."

"But we're starved dad, and I'm worn out. Can we have a bite of something before we go?"

"There's not a crumb to be had, Charlie, unless you get it yourself."

All the children picked themselves up slowly, lacking energy to do much else, and went.

He addressed me again. "I don't know if you know, but there's surface coal on the moors over the back of the big house where you work – just need to dig forit. There's no coal coming out of the mines, so that's the best we can do."

"I understand, Jimmy. We must be going now….. John."
I looked towards John to see if that was OK. He nodded.
Before we go, I must use your toilet.

"…. Oh, you mean the jetty. It's out at the back."

Page 114
"Jimmy, move yourself, fetch a bucket. It's the man with
the water".

Page 116
"It has led to a mob of colliers and others going around the
district forcibly stopping men from working at the pits. It
has been reported in the papers. Of course, the papers are
all for Mr Sparrow, they think he's not at fault, he's in the
clear. Trouble is, that most folk do not want to strike, they
cannot afford to be out of work. Everyone's scared.

Pages 117 - 118
"Mr Meigh and the other magistrates called out the yeomanry
and troops a couple of days ago. They set up on Hanley race
course. That fairly defeated the strikers and some of them
returned to work. The colliery owners promised to look at
their wishes, so the bands of men, demanding money with
threats of violence, went home. But the owners did not pay
them anyattention and, in consequence, two pits came out
and I hear there was trouble in Burslem yesterday."

"Yes, I heard about it…. Jimmy mentioned the Chartists.
Who are they and how have they become involved in all
this, John?"

"Ah well, dear, the Chartists got together a People's Charter in 1838 – you have the pamphlet Jimmy gave you. That was presented to Parliament with all of our wishes, but Parliament rejected it. But they have not given up and the magistrates are certain the Chartists have instigated all of these goings on, saying they have put spies out on the military. The Chartists have been spying at rallies and meetings, getting people rowsed up. They want to offer men, and some women, the opportunity, with this Charter, of getting a vote, getting a say in who is elected to Parliament – as they call it 'the vote and more to eat' and the chance to stop 'dying to live'. They want to present another Charter to Parliament.

"Ah, these are the three Poor Law Commissioners in London, ducky." He replied.

Page 119
"What's a Sacred Week?"

"Ah, that's their way of saying they want to organise a strike. They got together a petition this year of ten thousand signatures. I believe they have got guns and pikes – they are preparing for war. They are also telling people to apply for poor relief. I know, in Burslem, up to give hundred new applications for assistance are seen every day. They cannot cope."

"About 5,000 miners are on strike at present. They are demanding a pay rise an eight-hour day, free coal to be paid in cash and that five nights' work should be payed as six days."

"I'd like to go back some time to Hanley, John. Jimmy mentioned the Chartists would be speaking again soon. Do you think it is possible we could attend one of those meetings?"

"We'll see, dear. See if we can work a day when there's a speech planned and we can get time off"

Pages 160 - 161

The rector's furniture and his valuable collection of rare books fuelled a bonfire. Furniture was thrown out of the windows onto a fire in front of the house. Someone was seen demolishing the woodwork around the windows while others were seen breaking bedroom furniture by banging the pieces together. and the house itself also was ignited. Someone, who hearing this, remarked, "he well deserved it. It was he who'd made the crass remark about how we poor people should use grass and leaves to make tea if we could not afford to buy it from the shops. Good riddance to him, that's what I say."

Pages 165 - 166

So we were there the next morning, Tuesday, 16th August 1842, at 6am. There was a lot of laughter and high spirits amongst the crowd. I could see that quite a few were still drunk from the night before. Listening to people there is seems that the violence hadn't ended last night. Cooper had closed his meeting at dusk and a drunken group, decided to make their way to the Rev Aitkins' house, who was on the Board of Guardian at Stoke Workhouse, along with Rev Vale. They knew he had wine cellars and they wanted more. Someone called Edward was shouting out, "Thomas

Owen – he's our man, he's our leader – up went 'is orders – 'We are the boys, we cando it' – so we all charged in after him." Rev Aitkins' wine cellars were soon emptied and consumed by the mob, which consisted of men, women and boys. Aitkins. was left without even the walls to his house, with the whole building reduced to rubble. Thomas Owen had gone in, as their leader, and knocked the window sashes out and began throwing furniture out onto the fire in front of the house. Everyone else had followed suit. Someone else shouted out that he'd got several plated candlestick from the house. Someone called Joseph Whiston, who I found out was a potter and Methodist lay preacher was claiming, "It was me who was the first one to set fire to his house. They're a mean bunch of people. They care nothing for the poor buggers under their care. I did it in the Lord's name, the Lord's judgement on them.

Page 170
I saw a man striking out at the dragoons, using a large stick – "That's Cogsey Nelly" John said beside me. "He's one of the three who climbed the Town Hall tower and broke the new clock. He was imprisoned but he got broken out."

Page 178
Whan Aw, I hold onto it when I'm feeling a bit worried. I say a little prayer in the hope she's looking down on me and can protect me."

"Is it a religious symbol or a cross?"

"No, dear, it's a ring. My wife's wedding ring. I put it on a chain around my neck, so she'll always bay with me."

"I didn't know you'd been married, John, what happened to her?"

"She died of cholera, about five years ago, 1st October 1837 to be precise. I nearly died with her, but didn't in the end. She was the love of my life, my Alice. I still miss her."

"Oh, how sad for you, John."

"Our names are on it. I got it engraves, it says – Alice and John."

Page 207
Wake up Jane, come on. There's trouble at the house".

Pages 208 - 209
You're still filthy rich, and care nothing for the likes of us." and similar cries were being shouted out as Mr Meigh tried to state his case.

I then heard John's voice rise above the tumult, "Mr Meigh's a fair man. He's done alright by me. He looked after me when I was sick and could not work. He looks after all of his people. He's a good man. Get going home. You've turned on the wrong one here."

Someone shouted from the crowd, "What are you going to do – fight all of us, by yourself?"

Page 210
Just then someone shouted out. He'd seen the outdoor raiments apparently drying in that front room. "Hey lads,

hold up, he's got a bloody army in there. He trying to trick us." The mob paused, its resolution broke, its solidarity crumbled and away it began to drift, slowly and then with increasing rapidity as rain drops, once more, began to blow over Ash Bank.

"Have you seen Jane?" Mr Meigh asked John.

"Why, she was with me a moment ago….. She's not well." I could sense John trying to work out what to say, hedging his bets, trying to get an idea of what Mr Meigh knew.

"I'm angry with her. She's left my wife all on her own, to fend for herself, with no offer of assistance, so she could not leave her room."

John was thinking on the spot now, "I'm sorry, sir, but she's not been well all day. She's running a fever. I'm sorry I could not get to Mrs Meigh.

He went inside for a second and came out with a load of leaflets and papers that we'd picked up on our visits to the Chartist meetings. He threw them at him "So, you're nothing to do with these rioters and so-called Chartists? I found them in your rooms?"

"They were from my brother in Tunstell. We went there to visit as Jane wanted to know more about the Chartists, but we've had nothing to do with these rioters. We've been here all the time."

"She's been in the toilet at the back, caught bad, a bit sickly. I got wet flannels for her head. Cleaned her up, given her something to drink. I think she's fallen asleep now."

"So, you haven't been near Burslem today, it's just that someone looking very much like Jane has been seen there, among the rioters?"

"No, sir, certainly not, sir – must have been someone who looks like her – mistaken identity."

"And what have you done to your hand, John. I see it is bandaged?"

"Oh, I cut myself, out chopping wood. Not much but means I have not been able to do much labouring, and I would not have been able to help Mrs Meigh downstairs."

"Don't talk like that, dear. I did not do anything I didn't want to do. Don't worry."

"I really believe that Mr Meigh, if he'd known the truth about today, and if he had seen us together, it would have sent him over the top. You know he has made advances to me. I believe he would have gone into a jealous rage and I don't think it is beyond him to have taken his rage out on you, on both of us, physically.

"Yes, I had to think on my feet, put on the spot as I was, especially when he produced those Chartist pamphlets. A cunning deceit. I was frightened he would be grabbed hold of to try to physically hurt me."

"What do you mean? Don't be daft. I want you to stay, Jane. I believe you know I love you too." He kissed me, tenderly. "If you'll have me, I want to wed you. Will you marry me, Jane? We can fend for ourselves – get away from here and Mr Meigh, run away."

Pages 214 - 215
"Look, she's weeping. Doctor, she must be in pain. Do something, please."

"I've given her some Laudanum to give her some relief, she should be coming round soon."

"Jane, Jane, I'm here for you. You're safe now. It's me, John. Wake up please."

The voice sounded like John's and he said, 'It's me, John'. Am I dead? Am I alive? What year am I in? Should I try to open my eyes? I'm scared.

"There's nothing to be frightened of – I'm here. Come on – open your eyes. That's my girl – my wife to be."

It is John, he's calling me his wife to be. "John." I heard myself say, barely audibly.

"That's it, Jane. It's me, John. You can do it. Open your eyes."

It's good to have you back, darling girl."

Lightning Source UK Ltd.
Milton Keynes UK
UKHW04f0846310718
326548UK00001B/14/P